Creating Responsible Learners

PSYCHOLOGY IN THE CLASSROOM: A SERIES ON APPLIED EDUCATIONAL PSYCHOLOGY

A collaborative project of APA Division 15 (Educational Psychology) and APA Books.

Barbara L. McCombs and Sharon McNeely, Series Editors

Advisory Board

Sylvia Seidel, National Education Association
Debbie Walsh, Chicago Teachers Union, American
    Federation of Teachers
Ron Brandt, Executive Editor, Association for Supervision
    and Curriculum Development
Isadore Newton, University of Akron
Merlin Wittrock, University of California, Los Angeles
David Berliner, Arizona State University
Noreen Webb, University of California, Los Angeles

Series Titles

*Becoming Reflective Students and Teachers With Portfolios
    and Authentic Assessment*—Paris & Ayres
*Creating Responsible Learners: The Role of a Positive Classroom
    Environment*—Ridley & Walthers .
Motivating Hard to Reach Students—McCombs & Pope
*New Approaches to Literacy: Helping Students Develop Reading
    and Writing Skills*—Marzano & Paynter

In Preparation

Teaching for Thinking—Sternberg & Spear–Swerling
Designing Integrated Curricula—Jones, Rasmussen, & Lindberg
Effective Learning and Study Strategies—Weinstein & Hume
Positive Affective Climates—Mills & Timm
Dealing With Anxiety in the School—Tobias & Tobias

Creating Responsible Learners

The Role of a Positive Classroom Environment

Dale Scott Ridley and Bill Walther

AMERICAN PSYCHOLOGICAL ASSOCIATION | WASHINGTON, DC

Published by
American Psychological Association
750 First Street, NE
Washington, DC 20002

Copies may be ordered from
APA Order Department
P.O. Box 2710
Hyattsville, MD 20784

In the UK and Europe, copies may be ordered from
American Psychological Association
3 Henrietta Street
Covent Garden, London
WC2E 8LU England

Typeset in Berkeley and Arbitrary Sans by KINETIK Communication Graphics, Inc., Washington, DC

Printer: Braun-Brumfield, Inc., Ann Arbor, MI
Cover Designer: KINETIK Communication Graphics, Inc., Washington, DC
Technical/Production Editor: Sarah J. Trembath

Library of Congress Cataloging-in-Publication Data
  Ridley, Dale Scott
      Creating responsible learners: the role of a positive classroom
      environment / Dale Scott Ridley and Bill Walther.
      p.   cm. — (Psychology in the classroom)
      Includes bibliographical references (p.   ).
      ISBN 1-55798-295-3 (alk. paper)
      1. Classroom management—United States. 2. Classroom environ-
      ment. 3. Self-control—Study and teaching (Secondary)—United
      States—Case studies. I. Walther, Bill. II. Title. III. Series.
  LB3013.R525 1995
  371.1'024'0973—dc20   95-22563
                                                             CIP

British Library Cataloguing-in-Publication Data
A CIP record is available from the British Library.

Printed in the United States of America
First Edition

TABLE OF CONTENTS

PREFACE

Much is said these days about the poor quality of our schools. It seems that almost every day one can hear a new story in the press about the ills of the American educational system. Maybe the observers of our current system of education report mostly negatives because that is what they expect to find, and one may wonder how many press representatives are looking for the success stories that occur daily in our schools. If people choose to focus only on the bad, they can find plenty of which to speak. There are social issues that affect certain students, such as poor living conditions, frequent moving, low family income, poor nutrition or health, family instability, lack of positive role models, gangs, drug abuse, and violence. In school environments funds are often limited, and time and resources taxed. Teachers may find their decision making stymied by various conflicting ideological groups in the school or community, or feel pressures to "teach to the test" instead of focusing on meaningful student learning. Teachers are also subject to curricula and school policy dictated by administrators in a top-down manner that encourages them to be robots instead of creative thinkers and facilitators, as well as growing classroom sizes that limit the development of personal bonds. What businesses in our country deal with these kinds of pressures and still profit?

In all of the negative, however, there exists a multitude of positives. Like early spring flowers blooming in the snow, there are many teachers and schools that refuse to be held down by a heavy blanket of negativity. So what of the successes? If one only looks, he or she will find teachers and school faculty who succeed daily because they care too much to quit. One could even find teachers who go beyond the call of their duty—those who care enough to do special learning activities outside the classroom, who stay after school to help students who are behind, or who take the time out of busy schedules to get to know students personally. These educators truly want to create classrooms that are places of responsibility and meaningful learning.

We acknowledge these committed teachers. They renew our faith in the possibility for positive change. It is in this spirit that we offer this book—a book for teachers at all levels about creating positive and meaningful environments for learning and self-directed behavior. Although the recommended teaching strategies in the book are based on current research and practice, we also confide our belief that the suggestions in this book are most likely to work for teachers who have maintained their faith in students, even in the face of foreboding appearances. We cannot emphasize enough our belief in the importance of this sense of faith in students. Armed with a continued faith that all students can and want to learn, we hope that the strategies in this book will help more teachers move a step closer to creating positive learning environments that break through the appearances of negativity.

D. Scott Ridley
Bill Walther

introduction

As a student, what was the best class that you ever had? What made it so meaningful to you? Most of us can picture that time and place in our education when things just seemed to be right. Maybe learning was fun, or maybe we felt confident and in control. In spite of the years gone by, most of us can remember our teachers in these classes—if not their names, at least their faces and their mannerisms.

For most of us, one of our positive memories is likely to be that the teacher cared whether we, as individuals, learned or not. Most of these memorable teachers were fun to be around, even though they may have gotten fed up with the class from time to time. But through it all, and without many students realizing how, these teachers were able to maintain not only their sanity but also a positive classroom environment: a place of responsibility and meaningful learning.

As adults and teachers looking back on these excellent educators, it is easy to be in awe of their accomplishments. People wonder, "How did he or she do it? How can I make a difference like that for my kids?" This book is a small contribution to those teachers striving to make a difference in the lives and education of their students. More specifically, practical, research-based ideas are provided for helping teachers to make their classrooms places of responsibility and meaningful learning.

The classroom must be a place of responsibility because, in order to be successful in school and in the world, students must learn to manage their own learning and behavior. Classrooms must also be places of meaningful learning so that students can develop a genuine appreciation for life-long learning. Teachers must foster this appreciation for learning—which may be important in a quickly changing world—by facilitating learning experiences that are perceived by students as having the potential to make a difference in their lives.

There are two broad and related themes that serve as the foundation for the suggestions in this book. First, teachers can create meaningful and positive classroom learning environments by using teaching strategies that meet students' basic affective/motivational needs—fundamental human needs that are essential to openness and learning. Second, teachers can create more responsible students by using a student-directed form of discipline that teaches them how to make better choices.

There is also a close relationship between positive learning environments and student discipline. Many teachers know from experience that discipline problems can be minimized by making classroom learning experiences appropriately challenging, relevant, and fun. Thus, creating a meaningful and positive learning environment may be a proactive approach to discipline.

Experienced teachers know that it is easy to talk about proactive discipline through a positive classroom environment but that such a program can be extremely difficult to implement. Not wanting to think about and plan for this book from behind our own rose-colored glasses, we thought it would be helpful to ask some middle school teachers about the ways that they created positive classroom environments. Below are some of their comments:

> There are a few ways that I try to create a positive environment. Here they are: First, in terms of maintaining class attention and control, at the beginning of each class I ask students to turn their attention to me and to sit quietly in their assigned seats. Inevitably, as in any meetings, even with adults, there are a few who keep talking, not with the intent of being disruptive, but are just meeting their needs for fun. With that in mind, I do not often have to raise my voice, but just stand with my hands clasped, looking either at them or at the carpet with a thoughtful facial expression (Honest!). This avoids me having to yell or rant and rave at them to be quiet and try to act their age.

> The second way that I create a positive classroom environment has come with time and experience in the classroom. Basically, when a student hasn't followed my directions, I remind that student with the usual, "What's the rule?" If, however, a student continues to disobey my directions, I try to follow the maxim to "Try to put out the fire with the least amount of water possible." It's a general platitude, to be sure, but it

does prevent a lot of pointless power struggles that, bluntly speaking, will often just escalate into a contest, in which both will always lose.

The third way I try to create a positive classroom environment is to occasionally laugh when a student says or does something disruptive. Obviously this depends on the time, student, and situation, but laughing defuses tension, prevents hostility, and relieves a lot of stress.

□

I create a positive classroom environment by first and foremost smiling (not the fake kind). Also, using the student's name helps. Listening to the student when it's important to them that you listen. A little teasing helps and too much teasing hurts. It's a fine line to walk. For me, remembering that everyone does what they do for very good reasons, even if I don't understand the reasons, helps me to create a more positive classroom environment.

I think that a positive classroom environment comes down to treating people the way you'd like to be treated (you know, that "Golden Rule" stuff).

□

I have always believed that students cannot learn in a classroom unless they are comfortable first. I have made it a practice to greet students as they enter my classroom and find out how they are feeling so I can understand their behavior better. My classroom is made as comfortable to the students as possible. My students understand that they are free to move around, yet also learn when it may not be appropriate to do so. I feel that I have a very close relationship with my students, but also maintain the student–teacher status. I am not afraid to make mistakes, and my students then feel comfortable with theirs.

During class time I try to focus only on the positive. My statements to students are carefully thought out (most of the time), and I won't tell a student they are "wrong." I will guide them to the more accurate answer instead. This keeps the positive flow and allows them to feel success.

Outside of my classroom I also try to maintain close relationships. I will always take time to listen to a student when he or she wishes to talk. I go every day to the lunchroom and try to greet my afternoon students, which helps to set the stage for a positive afternoon. I'm sure there is a lot more that I do subconsciously. I believe that our students are the most important issues, not just our curriculum.

□

I guess the learning environment is positive when everyone is so engaged in the learning process that they forget they are obliged to be there. For this to happen, the topic has to be viewed as clear, interesting, and important enough to make personal mastery the goal. I guess even more fundamental than these factors is that learners must have a general feeling of safety in the class, and they must be confident enough in their ability that the prospect of failure doesn't rob them of their curiosity.

1 In what ways do you create a positive classroom environment?

Most of the teachers just quoted define a positive classroom environment from the perspective of the student. This seems sensible, but it is not how all teachers define a positive classroom. In the "real world" of teaching, many factors influence teachers' views about what constitutes a positive classroom environment. Teachers are influenced by their past experiences as well as the expectations of other teachers, parents, and administrators. These experiences and expectations may or may not lead a teacher to define a positive classroom environment from the perspective of his or her students. If students, teachers, parents, and administrators do not agree on which factors make up a positive classroom environment, to whom should the factors be tailored?

In our view the answer is simple: Tailor the environment to foster the learner's learning. This means that in creating a positive classroom environment the needs of students must be ranked above all others. Again, experienced teachers know that this is simple to say, but can be difficult to implement. Restricted budgets, large class rosters, state-mandated curricula, underprepared students, family-related problems, and other factors provide real obstacles that must be navigated. These obstacles contribute largely to the gap between what teachers want to make possible and what they are best able to provide.

Of course, these difficulties do not excuse teachers from striving toward the ideal. On the contrary, working to bring together our ideals (what we know) and our practice (what we do) is what a professional teacher's career is all about.

STATEMENT OF RATIONALE AND GOALS

Rationale

In a time when teachers face unprecedented obstacles to teaching and learning, the need to guide students in becoming self-directed and responsible learners is greater than ever. In this book, we share—teacher to teacher—practical, research-based ideas on how to create a more positive and meaningful environment for learning as well as ideas for teaching students to be more responsible.

Goals

When you complete this book you will

1. Understand the similarities and differences between students' and teachers' definitions of a positive classroom environment as well as the implications of these differences.

2. Understand a number of strategies for creating a positive classroom environment by meeting students' needs.

3. Have a theoretical and applied background on a student-directed approach to discipline that teaches students to make responsible choices.

4. Understand a number of strategies for fostering student self-discipline.

5. Have an understanding of the limits and obstacles that must be overcome to create a positive classroom environment and to shape more responsible students.

OVERVIEW OF THIS BOOK

To help readers achieve these goals, we first explore students' and teachers' attitudes concerning the factors that contribute to a positive classroom environment in Goal One. In Goal Two we address the issues of creating a positive classroom environment by striving to meet students' affective/motivational needs. We know a number of teachers who are experimenting with different strategies to determine what works best to improve students' attitudes about learning. Based on their teaching experiences and research, we share tips and methods for meeting students' affective/motivational needs.

In Goal Three the question of whether students have the capacity to regulate their own behavior in a classroom is addressed. We think it is possible for students to regulate their own behavior, but we are careful to present a realistic view of the limits in addition to the potential advantages of this approach to discipline. To present an accurate picture, we chronicle the actual and ongoing evolution of this method in a middle school where one of the authors is employed as a teacher, and we discuss the strategies that serve as the cornerstones of a student-directed approach to discipline. Finally, in Goal Four, we discuss some of the teacher- and school-level barriers that must be overcome to successfully implement the strategies presented in this book.

A number of self-directed activities for you and activities for students have been included to stimulate your thinking and planning. References for additional reading on some topic areas are also provided. We think that both preservice and in-service teachers will benefit from this book. The book should also be useful for self-study, for professional development workshops or discussions, or as a guide for staff development personnel looking for strategies for fostering meaningful learning and responsibility. After reading this book, we hope that teachers will have a few new ideas to try out in their classrooms. We encourage you to move slowly as you implement these ideas. Learning and mastery for teachers, like students, take time and persistence. As you read, reflect, and experiment, we encourage you to give yourselves the same kind of support and encouragement that you give your student learners.

goal one

Defining a Positive
Classroom Environment

In this chapter students' and teachers' attitudes concerning the factors that contribute to a positive classroom environment are explored. We found some important similarities and differences in how students and teachers define the factors that create a positive learning environment. Teachers need to understand these similarities and differences if they are to be effective in meeting students' classroom environment needs. The following review of student views on the factors that shape positive learning should help teachers better understand students' needs.

STUDENT VIEWS

A review of the many books and research articles on positive classroom environment and classroom management led to an interesting finding. Only a few studies mentioned anything about students' needs, attitudes, or perspectives on the issue of positive classroom environment. Instead, most of these resources jumped right into teacher strategies for managing the class in a positive and effective way. The absence of explicit information about student needs regarding a positive classroom environment may suggest a deficiency in the thinking of some educators. Research on motivation, however, has found that students, the consumers of our services, have specific needs and attitudes that must be understood and addressed (e.g., deCharms, 1983; Deci & Ryan, 1985; Maslow, 1970; Ryan, 1991; Schunk, 1991). The following list of motivational factors students may need or want in a positive classroom environment was compiled with these findings on motivation in mind.

Students want

◻ acceptance, a feeling of worth, and respect for their school and nonschool identities, for their personal interests, feelings, ideas, family lives, cultures, and so on.

◻ belonging and bonding with fellow students

◻ choice, shared ownership, and involvement in determining classroom direction

◻ personal responsibility, autonomy, and independence

◻ a positive personal relationship with teachers

◻ purposeful and challenging school work

◻ confidence in their ability to understand and learn

- active engagement and involvement rather than boredom

- creative work

- personal goal achievement

- fun while learning

- numerous opportunities for mastery

- recognition for effort and success

- trust

- variety in learning

- opportunities to work with other students as well as individually

- safety from being embarrassed or cajoled into learning

- understanding of strategies for learning and problem solving

- a "humanized" curriculum that connects their outside lives to what is being taught

- clear rules, procedures, and a classroom structure that makes the behavioral and learning expectations explicit

- detailed and accurate feedback

- willing extra assistance from teachers when necessary

- minimized classroom competition

- teachers with high but accurate expectations of their ability

- equity in teacher's treatment of students

This list does not represent the needs of every student, nor is it complete. It would be impossible to list every student's needs, yet this list does help teachers understand what many students need in a positive learning environment. Note that many of the needs are nonacademic. They relate to the student's identity, attitudes, emotions, and sense of personal control within the learning environment. The teacher's sensitivity to these personal factors is a key determinant of her or his ability to create a positive classroom environment. We will touch more on this later, but first let's explore teachers' views on the factors that contribute to a positive classroom environment.

1   In the space below describe the best class you ever had. Be sure to describe the things that made the classroom a good place to learn.

In the same way that the list of student needs cannot represent all students, the following list cannot represent all teachers' needs. As has already been discussed, teachers vary in their views of what contributes to a positive classroom environment. The list of teachers' needs was created with the intent to provide you with a representative list of factors teachers may consider to create a positive classroom environment. This list is based on the work of researchers who have studied teachers' classroom management needs and the creation of positive learning environments (e.g., Emmer, Evertson, Clements, & Worsham, 1994; C. S. Weinstein & Mignano, 1993).

Teachers want

☐ a physically safe environment

☐ cooperation among students and between teachers and students

☐ mutual respect among teachers and students

☐ a visually stimulating classroom environment

☐ positive personal relationships with students

☐ variety and innovation in instructional approaches (e.g., inquiry-based learning, alternative assessments, integrated units, technology use)

☐ student involvement in the class

☐ lower levels of competition among students

☐ a clear instructional focus and outcome

☐ clear classroom organization and structure

□ clear and fair rules, expectations, and treatment

□ supportive parents

□ a supportive administration

□ access to materials and technology

□ a sense of control over the direction and outcomes of the classroom

□ a sense of continuous improvement

The variables that define what many teachers consider to be a positive classroom environment are a mixture of instructional and classroom management factors, social–emotional factors, and professional growth and competence factors. Looking at the list, one can sense that these factors reflect the views of someone who has primary responsibility for managing the learning experience. The next section addresses the major similarities and differences between teachers' and students' perceptions of a positive classroom environment.

1 What other factors do you believe contribute to a positive classroom environment?

COMPARISON OF STUDENT AND TEACHER VIEWS

Clearly defined classroom rules, procedures, and structure are common desires of students and teachers. Like teachers, most students value a structure that promotes discipline in the classroom. They want to feel safe. If given the opportunity, most students will be quite detailed in stating the need for discipline. In fact, in one middle school[1] all students were asked if they saw a need for rules in the classroom, hallways, lunch room, bus lines, and so on. It was surprising how close students' ideas about effective discipline were to those of teachers. Results at this school match those of other research on student attitude toward discipline (e.g., King, Gullone, & Dadds, 1990). Understanding that most students actually desire firm and consistent discipline is an important point for teachers and administrators to remember when they plan how discipline will be implemented in their school.

Another area of similarity between students and teachers is the need for involvement in the classroom activities. Teachers want students to be involved, and students report that they prefer to be actively engaged rather than bored or passively involved in learning (Oldfather, 1993). However, there may be a difference in how teachers and students define the necessary conditions for student engagement. Similarly, both students and teachers consider variety in learning as important (Brophy, 1987). Furthermore, students cite a need to have a sense of belonging with their fellow students (Ryan, 1991). This student need seems to match the teacher's need for cooperation among students.

Students and teachers alike consider a positive student–teacher relationship to be an important factor in a positive classroom environment (Wubbels & Levy, 1993). Both students and teachers also cite the importance of mutual respect. In addition, research has noted that students also want their nonschool identities to be accepted, valued, and respected (Goodenow & Grady, 1993). Teacher acknowledgment of the student does not in itself fulfill this need (Kagan, 1990); it is hard work

[1]The middle school referred to is LaCima Middle School in Tucson. AZ. where coauthor Bill Walther is a teacher. This school is further discussed as a case study in Goal Three.

for the teacher to get to know and value the real person inside a student (e.g., their personal interests, feelings, family backgrounds, cultures). Although difficult for teachers to implement, respect for out-of-school identity is a high-priority need of students, especially those who are struggling on the margin (Schlosser, 1992). Finally, both students and teachers stress the importance of lowering classroom competition to help create a more positive environment (Johnson & Johnson, 1991). Competition does have some positive qualities. For example, many kids are motivated to win and thus pay closer attention to class activities. The downside of competition, however, is that a significant number of kids will resist engaging in competitive learning. They may fear embarrassment or damage to their images.

There are two major differences in the factors that students and teachers use to define a positive classroom environment. First, the factors important to students are much more personal and affective in nature than those valued by teachers. Second, both students and teachers need to feel a sense of personal control over the direction of the learning experience. Many times, however, this common need leads to more student–teacher conflict than consensus (C. S. Weinstein & Mignano, 1993). These two major differences become an important focal point of our argument that teachers are best able to create a positive classroom environment when they acknowledge and strive to satisfy students' basic affective/motivational needs instead of imposing their views on students.

1. What other similarities and differences do you believe exist in how you and your students define a positive classroom environment?

SUGGESTED READING

For further reading about the student and teacher factors that contribute to a positive classroom environment, we suggest the following:

Fisher, D. L., & Fraser, B. J. (1983). A comparison of actual and preferred classroom environments as perceived by science teachers and students. *Journal of Research in Science Teaching, 20*(1), 55–61.

Oldfather, P. (1993). What students say about motivating experiences in a whole language classroom. *The Reading Teacher, 46*(8), 672–681.

goal two

Meeting Students' Needs for a Positive

Classroom Environment

This chapter discusses six basic affective/motivational student needs that teachers must strive to meet if they are to create a positive and meaningful learning environment. The six basic needs are a synthesis of the student needs presented in Goal One. This list of needs, adapted from Glasser's (1986) control theory, delineates factors that drive the learner's affective/motivational state. Whether these needs are satisfied may determine whether a learner wants or feels able to engage in the learning activity.

An examination of the factors students use to describe a positive classroom environment quickly reminds us of how personal and emotional the learning experience can be. As teachers, we sometimes forget what it is like to be on the other side of the desk. However, if we put ourselves into the position of a learner, we can easily relate to the following needs:

□ emotional safety

□ fun (interesting and relevant subject matter)

□ self-confidence (a sense of competence)

□ belonging (connectedness)

□ power (personal control and recognition) and freedom (choice and autonomy)

Some teachers question whether they are responsible for or capable of meeting these student needs (Ovadia, 1994), and some teachers are not sufficiently motivated to do so. Yet, one of the basic themes of this book is that if teachers are to be successful in fostering meaningful learning, they must strive to meet these student needs. To help teachers meet this challenge, a number of research-based (and teacher-tested) strategies are presented.

Alternatives to attempting to meet student needs may be frustrating and less effective. Teachers often resort to less positive means of extrinsically motivating students, such as threatening poor grades or detention. Many of today's students are not as affected by threats as students from the past were; some have observed that it is getting harder to "scare" students at increasingly younger ages (Wlodkowski, 1991). Furthermore, many parents who experienced the "fear system of education" do not accept this approach for their children. Threats of poor grades and moral retribution also seem to lead to student resentment and future discipline problems. We have seen the more positive and effective choice is to explore ways to meet student needs.

1 Putting yourself into the position of a learner, which of the six affective/motivational needs do you relate to most? Explain your choices.

EMOTIONAL SAFETY

Create a Supportive Environment

An essential condition for a positive classroom environment is for the student to feel emotionally safe enough to take risks for learning (Brophy, 1987). Meaningful learning is often personally risky. We enter the learning process without knowing or understanding, and must be willing to acknowledge and possibly publicly expose this lack in order to gain new insights. As we get older, social pressure makes it harder for many learners to freely admit what they do not know (Dweck, 1986). The opportunity for meaningful learning expands when teachers are aware of these dynamics and create an emotionally safe environment where acknowledging one's lack of knowledge and mistakes in the process of learning is the norm (Ames, 1992). Following are some strategies for creating an emotionally safe and supportive learning environment.

1. *Model risk-taking in the process of learning.* This means admitting that we as teachers don't know it all, even though some students may think we should. Teachers can sometimes get caught up in feeling that they must be all-knowing. This expectation is a heavy burden for teachers and can have an impact on students' conceptions of how teaching and learning should occur (i.e., learning means listening to the "sage on the stage"). It is much healthier for teachers and more beneficial for students if teachers freely admit what they do not know. Admitting what one doesn't know doesn't have to be a negative experience; in fact, it can turn into a demonstration of the learning process itself. For example, if a student asks a question that the teacher cannot answer, he or she can say as much and, with the questioner, brainstorm resources that would be helpful to find the answer. This act demonstrates that even experts cannot know everything. More important, the approach illustrates a good way for the learner to gain desired knowledge. In this example, the teacher and the students become collaborators in the learning process.

2. *Create a warm, personal context where students are well-known and accepted.* This means being sensitive to and aware of students' lives outside of school. Such personal knowledge creates an important bond between teacher and student (Schlosser, 1992). Each individual becomes "three-dimensional" and is not restricted to the teacher–student role he or she plays out each school day. Personal knowledge of students also helps in the teaching process. When a teacher knows a student, he or she is able to draw on the student's experience to bridge the gap between course material and the student's prior knowledge and experience. Such personal connections also help teachers to make effective decisions about what knowledge or procedures must be made explicit to students, which is especially important with low-achieving students. Many low-achieving students need to be taught specific learning strategies (e.g., comprehension monitoring); rules (e.g., not to interrupt someone else's learning); and procedures (e.g., each student has a responsibility in a cooperative learning group) that govern the classroom (Schlosser, 1992). Some teachers, in the middle and high school grades, feel they should not have to "baby-sit" students by teaching them how to follow classroom or school expectations. However, teachers who are most effective at motivating struggling students are those who tend to believe that specific strategies, rules, and procedures must be taught (Schlosser, 1992), and teachers can demonstrate their caring by taking the time to teach learning-to-learn skills.

1 In what ways do you think your classroom environment is supportive?

2 What specific actions could you take to make the learning environment more supportive?

1 Learning can feel scary when you make mistakes or have to admit you don't yet understand new things. What happens to you when you make mistakes or don't understand material taught in this class?

2 Some students say they understand better when they feel the teacher cares about them, accepts them, and takes time to make sure they understand. Describe how your teacher makes you feel.

Make What You Do Interesting and Relevant to Students

Students need the time they spend in school to be interesting, fun, purposeful, and rewarding (Brophy, 1987). Imagine what it would be like to be required to spend more than 30 hours a week in a setting that you found boring and felt was a waste of your time. Because most people would suffer in such circumstances, many teachers strive to make their lessons interesting. Teachers know that it is hard work to make lessons interesting to students by connecting what they teach to their students' lives. The heroes, issues, fashions, and "language" of students change quickly, and it can be hard for teachers to keep up with these trends. We have found, though, that the more teachers know about students' "culture," the better able they are to relate class material to students' lives. Some teachers explain to students why a topic is relevant and then are disappointed to find that students continue to be unmotivated. However, simply telling students why certain information is important is only a partial step. Students have to be shown the relevance; they have to be sold on the value of the material. If that is not enough, teachers have to find a way to make the material interesting and relevant. Many older students are skeptical, so the job can be a hard one. How exactly do teachers make materials interesting? Exactly how depends on the students, but the following broad concepts and strategies are important first steps in the process.

1. *Adapt academic tasks to students' interests and language.* For example, a math assignment might require students to survey their peers to find out what percentage of them enjoys rap, rhythm & blues, reggae, rock, jazz, country, classical, gospel, or new age music.

2. *Provide information and ask questions in a way that intrigues students and makes them want to think.* For

example, when presenting a new scientific principle, begin by asking students to express their views about how this principle operates. (For example, if students pinch the skin on their hand and then release it, it will most likely recover more quickly than the teacher's. Ask students why they think this is so).

3. *Provide meaningful ways for students to get actively involved in a task.* The old saying that "we learn best by doing" is true for many learners. Consider how you can get students involved in seeing, hearing, touching, smelling, tasting, discussing, or acting out a concept. For example, in a psychology class, even complex concepts like the effects of personal comfort zones on communication can be role-played by having pairs of students stand at varying distances from each other while having a discussion.

Because students need to socialize, meaningful involvement is often achieved through allowing students to work together. The following are some examples of meaningful cooperative learning experiences. If you want students to practice writing more clearly in your English class, try this learning project using Legos. Have students pair up. Present one student with a structure created out of the Legos. Have this student write the steps involved in re-creating the structure, then provide his or her partner enough Lego pieces (plus extras) to duplicate the original structure by following the partner's written description. The students will learn that clear written communication is vital to the success of re-creating the structure. Or if you want students to become more meaningfully involved in your social studies class, try the following exercise. Rather than having students complete traditional reports on historical figures, have them become that figure. Students can research the figures and then provide autobiographical oral presentations to partners or to the entire class. Demonstrate the activity yourself. Dress up and really "get into" the role during your presentation. This will encourage your students to do the same.

4. *Be flexible and allow variation in your learning approach to accommodate learning process differences in your students.* Howard Gardner's (1991) work on multiple intelligence suggests that everybody has a preferred style of learning. Learners best create and demonstrate their understanding when they are able to use their preferred learning style. Thus, students' understanding may be maximized when their teacher allows them choices in acquiring and expressing understanding. For example, some students may prefer to work in groups while others choose to work individually. Some students may want to graphically illustrate a concept while others prefer to express the concept in a role-play demonstration or in a written report.

5. *Find ways to connect the curriculum with the world outside of the classroom.* Learning is often more relevant when one can see how knowledge or a skill is related to the "real world." For example, when studying the properties of acids, bases, and neutrals in science, a teacher might discuss the issue of acid rain. In addition to having hands-on activities like growing plants in varying amounts of vinegar solution to see the effects of levels of acidity on growth, the teacher might use newspaper articles, magazines, guest speakers, or videos on acid rain to make the topic come alive.

SELF-DIRECTED QUESTIONS

1 How interesting and relevant do you think your students find your curriculum?

2 What specifically could you change to make your curriculum more interesting and relevant?

3 How will you measure whether your idea(s) is (are) effective (e.g., What success indicators will you look for?)?

1 How important and interesting are the things you learn in this class? How do you think you'll be able to use what you're learning later on?

2 For your least favorite class, what types of activities would make the subject more interesting to you?

SELF-CONFIDENCE

Help Your Students Develop a Sense of Confidence That They Can Learn

It has been shown that if students do not believe they can do the work—even if they actually can—they are likely to fail and eventually stop trying to master the material (Bandura, 1986). Thus, even though a task may be interesting and relevant, there is no guarantee that students will meaningfully engage in the task if they think they will fail. What this means is that a teacher must not only work hard to make a task interesting, he or she must also consider ways to help students feel confident about succeeding. Again, some teachers may wonder if this is really necessary. Consider the consequences of not trying: A certain percentage of your students will feel confident in their abilities while others (a) worry more about saving face than really learning the material; (b) go half-heartedly through the motions of learning in order to stay out of trouble; or (c) act out their frustration, fear, boredom, or anger with inappropriate classroom behaviors or with silent passive–aggressiveness (Covington, 1992).

How can a teacher help to make students feel more confident? Can it be done with traditional grading procedures? Undoubtedly, having to issue grades often negatively influences students' confidence and motivation; yet, it is not likely that the current grading system will go away soon. For teachers operating within the existing framework of most classrooms, the following concepts and strategies should be useful.

1. *Be willing to give extra assistance if it is needed or desired.* Many students are afraid or embarrassed to ask a teacher for help (Covington, 1992). These feelings are sometimes related to peer pressure or to the student's perception that a teacher is unwilling or unable to offer extra help. Although we understand the impact of time limits and work overloads, we believe that offering

students extra assistance is an absolute and fundamental responsibility of the teacher. Learning is not a contest in which students compete to understand first or best; it is a process, and few students will meaningfully understand a new concept the first time it is encountered.

Willingness to offer extra assistance may mean making time outside of regular class hours to go over the materials with students. Many students are very sensitive to teachers' attitudes about offering extra help. If a teacher seems impatient, the student may be anxious or embarrassed and stop trying to understand the material. It is important to be patient and to look for different ways of helping students to understand concepts (e.g., watching a video, role-playing, or doing an outline or other hands-on activity). Offering extra assistance may also mean allowing students to redo assignments to achieve mastery, or modifying an assignment to better fit the student's skill level.

2. *Carefully check and monitor students' understanding on an ongoing basis.* Another fundamental role of the teacher is to continuously monitor what his or her students are understanding. This is a difficult aspect of the job of teaching. To continuously monitor understanding takes time and cunning (given that some students may be embarrassed and hide their lack of understanding). We believe that most teachers (including ourselves) have, room for improvement in this area. We know that the pressure to cover a great deal of material pushes many teachers to move too quickly. In many cases, this results in half-hearted checks of understanding outside of traditional end-of-unit testing. It also means that teachers are too often forced into accepting only the faster students understanding the material while other students fall further and further behind. Many slower students become apathetic toward learning and may become discipline problems.

If a teacher's goal is to foster confident and engaged students, she or he must teach for understanding—even if that means reducing the volume of curriculum and the pace of instruction.[2] A teacher must also actively and

[2]While some students work at a slower pace, advanced students can be challenged with peer-tutoring or enrichment projects.

continuously monitor what his or her students understand. This can be done in a multitude of ways, including allowing students to use thumbs up or down to indicate responses and response boards (personal slates) for written responses, monitoring student interaction in cooperative learning groups, assigning nongraded quizzes or written or verbal student surveys, reviewing student notes or group projects, and encouraging student responses. However the goal is achieved, teachers must be actively moving, monitoring, and modifying instructional methods to ensure student understanding.

It is also important to ask content-oriented questions that check students' understanding. For example, instead of asking vague questions such as "Does everyone understand the problems of the Lincoln administration?" ask students questions like "From the presentation, why do you think that President Lincoln wasn't very popular during his time in office?" If students aren't able to answer important content-oriented questions, repeat the material or have students help each other to find the answers to such questions.

3. *Don't embarrass or cajole a student into learning.* Some teachers believe that from time to time students need to be shamed into doing the right thing (Schlosser, 1992). We do not agree. The research on student motivation also doesn't support embarrassing or shaming students (Brophy, 1987). Many students already engage in failure-avoiding strategies—strategies for surviving a difficult learning experience without major embarrassment—such as low effort, making failure look like a virtue, procrastination, and academic cheating as a means of saving face (Covington, 1992). Teachers who embarrass, cajole, or shame students only exacerbate the problem of trading off real learning for face-saving.

4. *Give quick, accurate, and detailed feedback in a constructive and encouraging way.* This point is related to the teacher's proficiency in checking students' understanding. If the teacher is actively involved in monitoring students' understanding, he or she is also in a position to

offer students feedback on their understanding. The same obstacles apply (time limitations, large class sizes, overloads of job responsibilities), but we believe that communicating quick, accurate, and descriptive feedback is a fundamental requirement for effective teaching. Professional teachers desire accurate and detailed feedback to validate their efforts and to help them to continue to grow, and students are no different.

As teachers, it is not always easy to give feedback to students when they are wrong. Research on feedback, however, suggests that the most effective kind of feedback is a constructive explanation of why an answer is incorrect; this information allows students to better understand how they can correct their own errors (Bangert-Drowns, Kulik, Kulik, & Morgan, 1991). Therefore, teachers must take the time to carefully explain orally or in writing to students what is effective and ineffective about their work.

5. *Focus the goal of education on the process of learning (individual effort and understanding) rather than the product of learning (performance, especially comparative achievement levels).* The majority of teachers with whom we have discussed this point admit that they believe teachers should stress the process of learning, but usually end up stressing the product of learning in their own classes. Accountability pressures by administrators and parents; standardized tests; and competition among teachers, schools, and districts push many teachers to focus on test preparation and student performance (Flink, Boggiano, & Barrett, 1990). Learning for the sake and pleasure of learning is a distant or even naive ideal to some teachers. Yet, research by Ames (1992), Dweck (1986), and a growing body of other educational researchers demonstrates that students try harder, take more academic risks, do better, and are more intrinsically motivated in classrooms that stress the learning process, individual effort, and understanding instead of comparative achievement levels.

Examples of strategies that focus on the process of learning include mastery grading; reducing the emphasis on social comparisons of student achievement (i.e., grades known only by individual students and the teacher); involving students in self-evaluation of their own work (e.g., portfolio of best works for student analysis of progress over time); and allowing students to progress at their own rate whenever possible (e.g., weekly and daily work goals on class projects, helping students monitor their own progress). These types of activities do take time, but they pay big dividends in terms of more motivated students and meaningful learning (Ames, 1992).

6. *Teach students how to set and strive for their own academic goals.* One of the most effective ways of boosting the academic confidence of learners is to encourage them to set and meet their own goals (Schunk, 1991). The teacher must closely monitor this process because low-confidence learners many times set unrealistic goals that are either too high or too low. This type of unrealistic goal-setting can be another means of saving face (Covington, 1992). The teacher can help students effectively meet goals by encouraging them to set realistic but challenging goals that are moderately above past levels of achievement. Some teachers go as far as basing students' grades on the percentage of their goal achievement.

A good place to start goal-setting activities may be having students set daily seat-work goals. To provide some initial motivation, teachers could provide rewards (e.g., a homework pass) for successful students. In time, goal-setting can be connected to longer term projects, and rewards can be phased out as students learn to enjoy the intrinsic value of achieving their goals.

7. *Design tasks to shape students step by step in the direction of your ultimate expectations.* It could be said that the best way to teach someone is to "meet them where they are." This means that teachers must respectfully acknowledge the achievement level of the learner (Brophy, 1987). Again, time limitations, large class sizes, and overloads of job responsibilities make it difficult for

many teachers to address the learning needs of individual students. In many cases, lessons are taught to the class instead of to individual students within the class. Given the wide distribution of student achievement levels within any given classroom, simply teaching a lesson to the class at the average level of student achievement within the class presents the problem of teaching over the heads of some students and below the level of others.

Many students to whom we have talked say that they feel helpless in classrooms where the teacher is teaching over their heads and is not acknowledging their level of understanding. The goal of understanding does not seem realistic for students who are unrecognized and behind (Covington, 1992). Instead, most students in such circumstances consciously or unconsciously establish a goal of saving face.

Meeting students where they are might involve pretesting to establish students' achievement levels, followed by the processes of goal-setting and shaping. Individual learning contracts and goal-setting engage the student's commitment to put forth effort. Shaping is the process of offering the student a sequence of tasks (seatwork, project, homework) within the contract that increase in complexity in small steps toward a higher achievement level. Achieving a large number of smaller successes helps to build student confidence and encourages persistence over time, making the learner more willing to take on increasingly complex academic challenges (Brophy, 1987).

8. *Give students more than one chance to learn the material through a mastery grading approach.* Learning is not a contest, but a process. If we as teachers really believe this, we must make the time to adopt a mastery grading approach and a process view of learning. Both are important because without a process view of education, mastery grading may be viewed, by both students and teachers, as a monotonous requirement instead of an opportunity for real understanding and mastery.

1 How do you think your students would judge your ability to make them feel confident about succeeding in your class?

2 What specifically could you change to make students feel more confident about succeeding in your class?

3 How will you measure whether your idea(s) is (are) effective (e.g., What indicators will you look for?)?

1 Sometimes students do poorly because they don't think they can do work that they really can do. How confident are you that you can succeed in this class?

2 How does your teacher make you feel like you will be successful in the class?

3 What are two ways that the teacher could make you feel better about your work?

BELONGING

Help Your Students Feel Valued, Connected, and Respected

The need for belonging is a strong motivating factor for most human beings (Ryan, 1991). Adults feel personal satisfaction when they perceive themselves as valued contributors to the circles in which they move, whether they be family, social, church, work, or community circles. Educators know that children also have a need for belonging. Middle and high school teachers know how important peer approval is to adolescents. In fact, it has been argued that one of the major attractions of street gangs for adolescents is the need for belonging (Burke, 1991).

Teachers may or may not be surprised to hear how important teacher caring, acceptance, and respect are to students. In fact, many studies have shown that teacher support is one of the main predictors of students' attendance and engagement in school (e.g., Edmonds, 1986; Finn, 1992; Goodenow & Grady, 1993). In addition, this research has established a connection between students' sense of belonging in school (i.e., feeling accepted, respected, and supported by peers, teachers, and other adults in the school social environment) and academic motivation and achievement, behavioral patterns in and out of school, and school enrollment.

Sadly, many students report weak beliefs that they "belong" in their schools, that teachers and schoolmates respect and value them, and that their friends think that being in school is worthwhile (Goodenow & Grady, 1993). In fact, in an overview of a number of studies on "at-risk" students (Wehlage & Rutter, 1986), it was observed that the most frequent and consistent perception found among students was that their teachers did not care about them.

Before we start berating ourselves, let's examine the societal factors that may be contributing to many students' sense of alienation from school. The United States has one of the highest mobility rates of all the developed countries. It has been estimated that about one fifth of all Americans move each year (Kehoe-Schwartz, Scott, & Birman, 1994), which points to the number of school-aged children who may face this type of disruption to their lives. In studies by the Department of Education and Denver Public Schools (cited in Kehoe-Schwartz et al.,1994), it was found that students who changed schools four or more times by the eighth grade were at least four times more likely to drop out of school than students who remained in the same school. This was true even after taking into account the socioeconomic status of students' families. Students who change schools frequently were also more likely to be low achievers, repeat a grade, or have nutrition or health problems.

Data also show that students from low-income families or students who attend inner-city schools are more likely to change schools frequently (Kehoe-Schwartz et al., 1994). The strain of financial burdens and often oppressive urban living conditions combined with the stress of unplanned moves, breakups of friendships and family ties, and changes in living and school conditions take a toll on students. The toll taken is typically a reduction in the student's self-esteem, drive, hope for the future, and trust in others (Schuler, 1990).

In this bleak setting it is no surprise that gangs have flourished in the inner city. Researchers who have studied gang life (e.g., Burke, 1991) report that many adolescents enter gangs because they do not receive affection or gain a sense of belonging from a family.

Many schools are struggling as they learn to deal with more and more students who are experiencing poor living conditions, frequent moving, low family income, poor nutrition or health, breakup of family, lack of positive role models, gangs, drug abuse, and violence. In many cases, teachers have not been adequately prepared to deal with these overwhelming social issues. As a result, some teacher educators are advocating a curriculum for preservice teachers that includes reflective decision making/problem solving instead of traditional instructional techniques (Callen-Stoiber, 1991).

Many schools have also started to change to meet the needs of students from high-risk environments. For example, a number of inner-city schools in the Phoenix, Arizona, area have extensive before- and after-school programs for students and house a number of social service agencies on campus. A few even provide an on-campus health clinic for students whose families cannot afford health care.

In other cases, unfortunately, the school environment may actually contribute to the problems of at-risk students. Students from high-risk environments are typically less motivated to learn and thus do less well academically. An immense body of research dating back to the late 1960s has documented that in less effective schools, teachers have minimal expectations of students who are dealing with the social ills previously discussed (e.g., Rosenthal & Jacobson, 1968; R. S. Weinstein, 1989). This differential teacher treatment often separates low-achieving students from their more successful peers. Furthermore, because of these students' low academic achievement, they are often socially isolated from their peers through interclass tracking. Research has shown that tracking often creates a peer subculture of low-achieving students who are openly hostile to academic learning (Fordham & Ogbu, 1986). Such environments typically foster a sense of alienation from school life and increase the likelihood of withdrawal from school altogether (Finn, 1989). Because teaching groups of low-achieving students is extremely challenging, teachers must be very confident and committed to reach these students.

It has been observed that the classrooms and schools in high-risk environments are often overcrowded, structured around teacher control, dominated by competitive rather than cooperative academic tasks, and staffed by teachers who feel disempowered and removed from school policy (Fine, 1986). Negative learning environments like these are sometimes created because some school administrators believe that they must choose between a "get-tough" academic orientation or a "soft" social orientation (Ovadia, 1994).

Creating a socially oriented curriculum would entail balancing academics with extracurricular activities, moral education, self-esteem training, community work, fine arts tuition, and self-awareness education. With limited resources and histories of low achievement, many school personnel choose the get-tough approach (Ovadia, 1994). This philosophy may feed an impersonal and low-tolerance learning environment in which educators can easily excuse themselves for allowing alienated students to slip through the cracks (Calabrese, 1989).

In our view, the negative outcomes resulting from the get-tough approach are sad and unnecessary. We believe, and research supports, that a balanced academic and social curriculum (e.g., Crain, Mahard, & Norot, 1989) taught by committed, caring, and interpersonally warm teachers (e.g., Wubbels & Levy, 1993) can make a difference in almost any student at any level. Edmonds (1986) has even stated that an environment such as the one described here can be "so potent that for at least six hours a day it can override almost everything else in the lives of children" (p. 103). In challenging times such as these teachers must ask themselves, how can we as caring professionals help students feel valued, connected, and respected?

1. *Show students that you care about them as individuals independent of their academic attitudes and achievements.* In recent years, a number of research studies have provided evidence that caring teachers are more effective teachers (e.g., Wubbels & Levy, 1993). A study of more than a 1,000 ninth-grade students (Brekelmans, Wubbels, & Levy, 1993) found that teachers' interpersonal communication style was strongly related to both student motivation and achievement. "Hard" evidence like the Brekelmans et al. study reinforces ideas about teaching that students have thought about for years—it matters that teachers care about their students.

How can teachers better demonstrate their caring? Most teachers know how to personally connect with students. For example, a friendly hello at the door, a brief one-on-one conversation about things happening in a student's life, or a brief written note of encouragement can make a student feel that a teacher cares. Many times, however, the pressing and constant demands of the teaching profession narrows teachers' consciousness to a very business-oriented focus. Teachers may not stop caring, but may demonstrate caring sporadically. Thus, a key strategy for fostering students' sense of belonging is to strive to maintain a personal awareness of the need to express caring on a day-to-day basis. Educators striving to consistently express caring may benefit from a reminder. A cue card placed in a strategic location may help. For more disciplined individuals, a journal is a wonderful way of monitoring and noting progress in this area. Another idea is to seek from your students periodic feedback about your interpersonal skills. You could do this informally (e.g., asking student representatives) or formally (e.g., constructing a questionnaire that assesses student perceptions of your interpersonal skills).

As teachers experience successes with day-to-day awareness, other caring strategies are likely to follow. Additional caring strategies might include using students' names more in class; showing greater enthusiasm about being with the students (even late in the day, week, or year); risking more personal disclosures during teaching (e.g., relating self to students, smiling, or using more open body language); being a more active listener to what students have to say—even about the issues that may seem petty; or letting students know they have a supporter. It is important to make sure you include all students, even the quiet ones, the poorly behaved ones, and other students likely to be overlooked. It is also important to remember that building relationships with students takes time. This may be particularly true with the students who need a personal bond the most.

Students from high-risk environments or those who have had difficult experiences with past teachers may not trust your motives. You will have to be consistent and patient with these students. It is likely they will "test" your caring. We point out that caring is not antithetical to firmness. We see demonstrating caring and being firm as interrelated. Caring adults often set reasonable limits that help shape the social skills of developing children. It is important to have clear rules of interaction. For instance, the classroom of one of the authors has the following rules: (a) be respectful to yourself and others; (b) be responsible for yourself; and (c) make no excuses–take no excuses.

2. *Enact a family environment and code in the classroom.* If your classroom was your home and the students were members of your family, how would you talk to them and treat them? In one sense, your classroom is your home. (You certainly spend enough time there!) Think of your classroom as your academic home and adopt a "family" code. Consider some elements of a well-functioning family. (a) In such a family there is a known operating structure—consistent operating procedures and rules—that is predictable and fair. (b) The family functions with a degree of democratic rule so that each member has input into the functioning of the family. (c) Each individual in the family is a valued member. With membership comes an identity, respect, basic rights, earned privileges, and duties. (d) Finally, family members strive not only to meet their own basic needs and goals but also assist other family members in meeting their needs and goals. Family members protect and serve each other to help the family function effectively.

There are numerous ways of creating an effective family environment in the classroom based on each of these four elements. The first element is a known operating structure that is predictable and fair: Students need to understand your academic and social expectations and the learning processes and procedures in your class. Students also need to know the consequences of their behaviors. Behavioral consequences can be made explicit by listing classroom rules and expectations. Commitment to class rules can be fostered by allowing the entire class family to create the rules. Some family members will "pick up" on the operating structure and rules more quickly than others. Thus, students may need reminders, and, ultimately, those members who continuously violate the family norms must face logical consequences.

The second element of effective family functioning is a degree of democratic rule. Ask yourself if you are more committed to decisions that you helped make. Most people, including your students, are more committed to decisions they had a role in making. Often, however, teachers do not seek students' views about the direction of class activities. Some teachers may even believe that students have little or no ability to contribute to curricular decisions. Consider the potential advantages of involving students in teaching decisions.

Allowing students to help you create the classroom operating structure and rules enlists their assistance in implementing the rules. Allowing students to choose methods of demonstrating their understanding of academic concepts (e.g., oral or written tests, role-play or demonstration, portfolios, videotapes, or a special written research project) has the potential of greatly reducing students' anxiety about grades as well as increasing their motivation. Allowing a degree of democratic rule doesn't mean that a teacher is giving up control; he or she is simply sharing control with other family members to foster commitment to effective functioning.

The third element of effective family functioning—ensuring that each individual in the family has a valued role—is important because family members feel better and contribute more when they perceive that, in some way, their roles are valued in the family. There are many students who do not perceive themselves as valued members of their academic family. These students feel alienated and are, in fact, frequently differentiated from other, more successful family members.

Educators often say that 20% of the students cause 80% of the discipline problems. A number of educators are pondering what to do with these students. Some school faculty believe that because family members with discipline problems so severely disrupt the learning of others, they should be physically separated from other students. Indeed, there are some middle schools in our state that have grouped "trouble-making" seventh- and eighth-grade students together into classes, preventing them from having contact with well-behaved students. As educators we must ask ourselves if we would choose physical separation to discipline our own children in our homes. Teachers should strive to make each student a valued "family member."

Some teachers would say, "Yes, if my kids acted like some of the students in my class, I certainly might consider isolating them!" Frustrated teachers are justified in feeling this way, but there are other workable solutions that keep these challenging family members in the fold and help them to act more responsibly at the same time. Research suggests that disruptive students are better off if they are allowed to stay in the mainstream of school life, rather than in pull-out programs that only increase their isolation (e.g., Catterall, 1986).

EXAMPLE: MONICA RICHARDS A convincing testimony is the experience of Monica Richards (1987), a middle school teacher in Kentucky, who wrote about her learning experience with challenging students. In her article, "A Teacher's Action Research Study: The 'Bums' of 8H," this teacher explored the question, "How am I going to motivate a group of students who do not want to learn?" Richards chronicled the growth of her own awareness of how she aided and abetted the problem of rowdy, unmotivated student behavior. By asking the students in her sixth period class to join her in a self-study of motivation to learn, she observed the students in new ways. To her surprise, over the course of the experiment, the students contributed to learning on an intellectual and motivational level much higher than she ever thought possible for them.

The experience contributed much to the teacher's learning. Richards stated

> Clearly, I had wasted many days assuming 8H was incapable of deep reasoning. I was guilty of letting their outer appearance and low academic ability sway my judgment. I had underestimated them; I found that they were capable of mature

thoughts. I soon came to realize that they not only needed but also appreciated a teacher who was knowledgeable and caring. (Richards, 1987, p. 71)

Teachers are often guilty of allowing outer appearances and low academic ability sway their judgment. Beliefs about certain students' low academic potential guides teachers to unwittingly disengage from these students, thus rejecting them as valued members of a family of learners. When students learn to undervalue their own academic identities, a self-fulfilling process is set into place (R. S. Weinstein, 1989), which often encourages students to dodge responsibilities and make trouble.

Monica Richards learned that when "troublemakers" were treated with genuine respect and challenged with duties and higher academic expectations, they responded. In her view, the hardest part was involving these students in the exploration of the problem and opening her mind to her own contributions to the problem. Richards borrowed from Holt (1970) to describe her feelings, "Most of us do not like to be surprised about the world, to find that it is very different from what we had supposed. We like even less to be surprised about ourselves" (p. 69).

Our challenge as teachers is to maintain our faith in students, even in the face of foreboding appearances. How? Talk to each student honestly about his or her effort and potential. Tell students and believe that they can and will succeed. Don't let anyone drown; keep trying to actively reach out to and work with students until they succeed or you run out of time. Find something positive that each student can contribute to your academic family and tell others about it. Don't allow yourself to become hardened, uncaring, or cynical about student failure. Be willing to let your heart be broken. Pretend each student was your only child.

The last element of a successful family is that members protect and serve each other. Many educators have seen classrooms where students appear to have little concern for one another. However, this does not have to be the case. Many teachers are discovering the benefits of peer-tutoring and cooperative learning activities—the next strategy for fostering students' sense of belonging.

3. *Use cooperative learning activities to foster socialization, networking, and connection among students and their peers.* Most teachers have been exposed to methods of involving students in group learning projects. Years of research on cooperative learning demonstrates the numerous academic and social benefits to students (e.g., Johnson & Johnson, 1991). Cooperative learning has been documented to contribute to students' social development and the quality of their peer relationships, which helps students feel valued, connected, and respected (Johnson & Johnson, 1991). In their interaction with peers, students directly learn attitudes, values, skills, and information unobtainable from adults. Cooperative activities provide students with peer support as well as opportunities and models for prosocial behavior. An important outcome of cooperative learning is that students learn to view situations and problems from perspectives other than their own. Perspective-taking is one of the most critical competencies for cognitive and social development (Johnson & Johnson, 1991).

We suggest that you try a variety of grouping methods. For example, you might sometimes allow students to pick their own groups, and other times you pick. Or allow students to pick one or two group members while you assign the others. Middle school and high school students sometimes enjoy being assigned into groups by random or systematic category assignments like makes of cars, types of flowers, names of states, musical instruments, by matching playing cards, and so on. Teachers can be creative here. We have found that the socialization benefits previously discussed are enhanced by frequently changing groups during learning activities.

4. *Use class meetings to discuss personal and academic issues.* The classroom meeting[3] is a student-led forum that allows participants to discuss issues of importance. Glasser (1969) has suggested that classroom meetings

[3]This strategy will be discussed in greater detail in Goal Three of this book.

teach students to (a) communicate with each other, (b) think about various sides of an issue, and (c) make decisions. Success with this forum comes when students learn to take responsibility for their thoughts and actions. Thus, it is important that teachers foster a sense of student ownership and self-regulation for these meetings (e.g., selection of topics, management of the behaviors of the participants, evaluation of the productivity of the meeting).

5. *Involve students in nontraditional learning activities that allow them to see each other and the teacher in a different light.* We know that students sometimes see teachers as almost machine-like. This might be due in part to the fact that students don't often see teachers involved in other human activities like eating, playing, laughing, and maybe even learning. This is a limitation because when teachers are perceived as nonfeeling, the opportunities for personal bonding and mentoring are reduced. Learning becomes less "real" in sterile and impersonal educational environments.

Research suggests that learning activities are most potent when they are meaningful and personalized to the learners (Brophy, 1987). Personalized learning means that an activity engages emotions and penetrates social self-presentation facades. To create a meaningful and personalized learning environment, teachers must provide a variety of learning activities that move students a safe distance out of their intellectual and emotional hiding places. In the state of mind that personalized learning fosters, students are more excited about making sense out of something new than they are worried about making fools of themselves (Ames, 1992).

How can teachers help students achieve this state of mind? Specifically, nontraditional learning activities like role-playing, reciprocal peer teaching, autobiographical exchanges among students, field trips, school-sponsored extracurricular activities, and show-and-tell of personal hobbies break up predictable classroom routines and help students and teachers to better appreciate each other's humanity.

6. *Give students responsibilities in the school.* Some researchers believe that student motivation and achievement has suffered in recent times partially because the curriculum has become detached from vocation (e.g., Collins, Brown, & Newman, 1989). In earlier times, many children learned the trades of their parents as apprentices. Because education was nested in day-to-day life, it was thought to be more meaningful than it is today. Another outcome of the separation of vocation and education is a reduction of duties of children and adolescents. Children in previous generations often had daily chores or other responsibilities.

Today, many children lack routine duties that may help them to develop skills, a sense of responsibility, and personal character. For this reason, some schools have begun to offer student "jobs" within the school (Shoop, 1990). Student jobs may be a journalist on the school newspaper, lab assistant, teacher's aide, and so on. Some middle schools in our state have adapted a microeconomy system. Students in this type of system seek jobs and earn salaries, pay bills, bank, invest, own businesses, and so on. In many cases, subject area instruction is tied to achieving success in the microeconomy. For example, students in math class may be motivated to learn about calculating percent of interest earned on potential investments.

In addition to learning activities that are connected to the day-to-day lives of adults, students may gain a sense of positive identity and belonging with these school responsibilities. These nonacademic roles may also help students to see the school in new ways. Instead of simply seeing schools as sites of intellectual drilling, students may begin to understand the social organization, including such themes as collaboration, teamwork, and personal dependability (Shoop, 1990).

1 How do you think your students would judge your ability to make them feel more valued, respected, and connected to you and other students in your class?

2 What is one thing you could change to make students feel more valued, respected, and connected?

3 How will you measure whether your idea(s) is (are) effective (e.g., What indicators will you look for?)?

1 Pretend this class is a family. Describe your place in this family. Do you feel accepted? Do you feel like you belong here?

2 What are two ways that the teacher could make you feel more like you belong and are an important member of the class?

POWER AND FREEDOM

Develop Students' Ability to Make Choices and Exercise Responsibility

Many students desire a sense of personal responsibility, autonomy, and independence (Deci & Ryan, 1985). They also consider having choices, shared ownership, and involvement in determining classroom direction related to a positive classroom environment (Brophy, 1987). As teachers, it may be hard to believe that some students want to take personal responsibility for their learning. Sometimes it seems that students want anything but responsibility; yet, students and teachers may simply have different conceptions of how the learning experience could be conducted. Furthermore, as discussed in Goal One, both students and teachers need a sense of control over the direction of the classroom. Students and teachers are often at odds about who should have control of the learning experience (C. S. Weinstein & Mignano, 1993).

We believe that today's teachers get mixed messages about who should be in control of the learning experience. Some educators (e.g., Ridley, McCombs, & Taylor, 1994) say teachers should make students more self-directed, responsible, and active learners (implying that teachers should share more classroom control with students), whereas other educators (e.g., Hunter, 1991) continue to stress the need for firm teacher direction, structure, and control. These mixed messages may be a result of the fact that the American educational system is in a slow transition from a behavioral teacher-centered orientation ("straight row, everybody-gets-the-same-thing" approach) to more of a social–cognitive learner-centered orientation ("shared control, more individualized education" approach). Mixed messages can be confusing and frustrating, especially if school or district policy and evaluation criteria differ from a teacher's personal beliefs.

Again, encouraging meaningful learning means that teachers must understand and strive to meet student needs. Thus, in the case of students' need for control, we believe teachers must offer students choice and involvement in the direction of classroom processes, and allow them to share in implementation of class procedures, curriculum, and discipline. At the heart of shared control is the belief that students are truly capable of directing their own learning. We believe that teachers can successfully foster students' sense of personal responsibility, autonomy, and independence when they share classroom control and respect students as the self-directed learners that they already are.

You may wonder why we believe that students are already capable of being self-directed learners. We believe that (a) all learning is self-directed or self-regulated and (b) the learner is always in control of her or his learning (Ridley, 1991). Regarding the first point, self-regulated learning is more than the use of proactive learning strategies (e.g., paying attention, asking questions); it is the ongoing process of interpreting learning situations, setting and using goals, and behaving in ways consistent with achieving one's goal. To equate self-regulated learning with the use of proactive learning strategies, as some researchers do (e.g., Zimmerman & Martinez-Pons, 1988), overlooks the fact that a decision not to use proactive learning strategies can be as much a self-regulatory decision as the decision to use them. For example, it is possible that a self-regulating student may not be willing to participate in a class discussion because experience tells her or him that divergent perspectives are not valued.

The key to purposeful learning is to facilitate students' reflection on their ongoing, self-regulatory processes. Many students aren't aware that they are in control of their interpretations, goals, and actions in the classroom. When students start reflecting on their own thoughts, feelings, goals, and actions related to learning, their increased awareness can have a profound impact on how things look to them. We have seen reduced self-doubt, higher levels of intrinsic motivation, more student initiative and perseverance, and greater achievement.

Although attitudinal surveys of students suggest that students want more classroom control and responsibility (e.g., Midgely, 1991; Oldfather, 1992, 1993), we believe that many students would initially not know how to effectively manage the higher levels of autonomy and authority they desire. In our view, an immediate willingness or ability on the part of students to share greater classroom control and responsibility may not be realistic given that most students have been socialized to be dependent on their teachers (Ridley et al., 1994).

To foster students' willingness and ability to accept classroom control and responsibility, the teacher must (a) honor students' perspectives, needs, and capacities within the context of a supportive relationship, and (b) help students become more aware of their ability to be agents of their own thinking and learning processes (McCombs, 1993). The teacher must respect, encourage, and support students' roles as co-creators of the classroom learning experience. Once teachers believe this about the potential of their students, they become able to shape students' beliefs about their own potential to be self-regulators. When this happens, shared control is likely to flourish in the classroom.

The following are some specific suggestions on honoring students and facilitating their awareness of their abilities:

- Encourage students to state their honest views and ideas.

- Once students state their ideas, treat those ideas with respect.

- Listen to students as they state or imply their needs.

- Do not put students down if they are not at the same level as other learners.

- Encourage students to make their work high quality. Let them know that effort makes the difference.

- Ask students for input on curriculum improvement.

- Don't structure every assignment; ask students to create some assignments.

Whether learners are conscious of it, they are always in control of their own learning. It is true what has been said about being able to tame the body (i.e., behavior) but not the soul (i.e., learning, attitudes, and thoughts). Sometimes teachers think that because they direct the classroom activities, control the timetable for learning, decide the methods of instruction, and determine the consequences for student behaviors, they, not the students, are in control of their learning. However, students are always in control of their learning. Teachers can facilitate their learning only if students allow them to. Even when students are quiet, go through the motions, and do not create any waves, it is no indication that teachers are controlling their learning. Teachers can facilitate student learning only by giving up some of the false control they thought they had. This means giving up some of the control over the content, the timetables, the instructional methods, and the evaluation processes.

If forced to say how a teacher can best meet students' control needs we would say, "Give students shared decision-making authority and structure their environment loosely enough that they have choices to make." We quickly add, however, that you will probably have to teach students how to make effective decisions and exercise authority. This is due not necessarily to lack of maturity, but to the fact that many students get little training about how to make and implement responsible decisions.

Schlosser (1992) found that a teacher's willingness to teach students how to make effective decisions had a positive motivational impact on marginal students as well as a positive academic impact. Specifically, Schlosser found that high-impact middle school teachers were not only warmer interpersonally, but also taught learning-to-learn (e.g., note-taking and reading comprehension) and self-control strategies such as peer-mediation. Schlosser found that low-impact middle school teachers distanced themselves emotionally from their students and believed that students should already have these learning-to-learn and self-control skills. Low-impact teachers believed that by the time students reached the seventh grade they should be mature enough to be able to identify and comply with teachers' expectations. These low-impact teachers believed that they should avoid "babying the student…[or] holding the student's hand" (Schlosser, 1992, p. 135). Some teachers in Schlosser's study went so far as to describe their role as that of an enforcer. Low-impact teachers often used referrals and suspensions to motivate students who they believed were failing academically because they did not care enough or have the willpower to learn. Teachers must be willing to teach the learning-to-learn and self-control skills that students lack at any grade level. Teachers should not withhold these strategies from students as a means of "preparing them" for the demands of secondary education.

Below are several strategies for sharing control of the learning experience.

1. *Offer choices.* In most areas (e.g., content, instructional processes, evaluation, discipline) giving students choices can have a major impact on their commitment to invest energy into learning activities (Brophy, 1987). For example, allowing students choices in the way they demonstrate their understanding has the potential to greatly reduce students' anxiety and obsession about grades.

2. *Seek and respond to feedback from students.* Do you really know how students feel about the way you teach? Ask students what they like and don't like. Ask what you can do to help them be more successful. Ask them what they specifically want to learn about some topic taught in your class. Ask them what classroom activities would make learning more meaningful and fun. Once you receive the answers to your questions, talk to students about their ideas. Decide which ideas will be tried out.

Determine goals and indicators of good work. Also establish the behavioral rules for the activity. Listening to students and jointly creating some of the class activities will make them feel more invested in the quality of the outcomes.

3. *Establish classroom policy and rules with students.* When students are involved in creating the class rules, they are more committed to keeping them. Some teachers may be nervous about sharing the rule-making process with students; however, research studies confirm (e.g., King et al., 1990) that most students desire structure and order just like teachers. In fact, in our experience, students can set tougher rules than their teachers. Teachers can facilitate the rule creation process by prioritizing students' proposed rules and limiting their number to a few major concepts. Too many rules make it difficult for students to remember them.

4. *Use student-led learning activities in class.* Many educators believe that the days of teachers simply spitting out facts are on the way out (e.g., Prawat, 1992). Many teachers are discovering the importance of giving students the opportunity of discovering facts by themselves. This is not to say that lecture is bad; it isn't. It is absolutely necessary at times. But you should vary instructional methods—some lecture, some cooperative learning groups, some individual seat-work, some peer-teaching, some student presentations, some demonstrations, and some reciprocal teaching in groups makes for more stimulating learning. In all cases, it is important to be clear and to communicate the objectives of the lesson. Sometimes student-led learning activities can be so much fun that everyone forgets the instructional purpose of the exercise. It may also help to summarize what was learned after a lesson has been completed.

Student-led learning activities are being described in the research literature in other terms, such as the learner-centered approach, the New Zealand approach (Nuthall & Alton-Lee, 1990), and the constructivist approach. Perhaps the best summary of the teaching practices associated with these student-centered perspectives is that of Brooks and Brooks (1993). They suggested that constructivist teachers do the following:

- Encourage and accept student autonomy and initiative.

- Use raw data and primary sources, along with manipulative, interactive, and physical materials.

- When framing tasks, use cognitive terminology such as "classify," "analyze," "predict," and "create."

- Allow student responses to drive lessons, shift instructional strategies, and alter content.

- Inquire about students' understanding of concepts before sharing their own understanding of those concepts.

- Encourage students to engage in dialogue, both with the teacher and with one another.

- Encourage student inquiry by asking thoughtful, open-ended questions and encouraging students to ask questions to each other.

- Seek elaboration of students' initial responses.

- Engage students in experiences that might engender contradictions to their initial hypotheses and then encourage discussion.

- Allow wait-time after posing questions.

- Provide time for students to discover relationships between related ideas and create metaphors.

These types of student-led learning activities, like any new learning process, take time and effort to acquire. In fact, when first learning these activities, many teachers and students struggle with and question the validity of the new learning approach. In time, however, teachers who persist and who clearly communicate their expectations will be able to develop these new student-led learning activities to the point where they begin to pay dividends.

5. *Involve students in self-evaluation.* Asking students to reflect on their academic progress gives them a sense of responsibility and continuity about how they arrived where they are (Morgan, 1985). Asking students to evaluate their behavior helps them to understand when and whether certain behaviors are appropriate (Jones, 1987). This type of involvement helps students to understand that they are ultimately in control of many of their outcomes. When the task of evaluation is shared with students, teachers are also released from some emotional burden. Teachers may even be surprised to find out that students can be quite objective about effort and behavior.

Teachers might begin involving students in self-evaluation by having them record their learning behaviors (e.g., time spent practicing, number of assignments completed). In time, students can be asked to evaluate more complex aspects of learning (e.g., whether they met their goals, how much they have progressed in the various subject areas). The use of student portfolios serves quite well this more complex type of self-evaluation.[4]

[4]See *Becoming Reflective Students and Teachers With Portfolios and Authentic Assessment,* by Scott G. Paris and Linda R. Ayres.

1 How much classroom control do you think your students would say you share with them? In what ways do you share control?

2 What is one thing you could change in your classroom to give students more decision-making authority and the space to exercise it?

3 How will you measure whether your idea(s) is (are) effective (e.g., What indicators will you look for?)?

1 Some students want teachers to share more classroom control. For example, students may think teachers should give them more choices in determining what happens in the classroom. In what ways does the teacher in this class share control with you?

2 Do you think the teacher in this class should share more or less control with students?

3 What are two ways that you would share more (or less) classroom control with students if you were the teacher?

Additional Reading

For further reading about creating an emotionally safe learning environment, we suggest the following:

Ames, C. (1992). Classrooms: Goals, structures, and student motivation. *Journal of Educational Psychology, 84*(3), 261–271.

Brophy, J. (1987). Synthesis of research on strategies for motivating students to learn. *Educational Leadership, 45*(2), 40–48.

For further reading about creating a fun learning environment, we suggest the following:

Brophy, J. (1987). Synthesis of research on strategies for motivating students to learn. *Educational Leadership, 45*(2), 40–48.

Wlodkowski, R. J. (1991). *Motivation and teaching: A practical guide.* Washington, DC: National Education Association Press.

For further reading about helping students feel more confident about their ability to succeed in your class, we suggest the following:

McCombs, B. L., (1993). Strategies for assessing and enhancing motivation: Keys to promoting self-regulated learning and performance. In H. F. O'Neil, Jr. & M. Drillings (Eds.), *Motivation: Research and theory.* Hillsdale, NJ: Erlbaum.

McCombs, B. L., & Pope, J. E. (1994). *Motivating hard to reach students.* Washington, DC: American Psychological Association.

Wlodkowski, R. J. (1991). *Motivation and teaching: A practical guide.* Washington, DC: National Education Association Press.

For further reading about helping students feel more connected in your class, we suggest the following:

Calabrese, R. L. (1989). Student alienation and academic achievement. *Education Digest, 54*(9), 7–9.

Johnson, D. W., & Johnson, R. T. (1991). *Learning together and alone: Cooperative, competitive, and individualistic learning* (3rd ed.). Boston: Allyn & Bacon.

Richards, M. (1987). A teacher's action research study: The "bums" of 8H. *Peabody Journal of Education, 64*(3), 65–79.

For further reading about developing students' ability to make choices and exercise responsibility, we suggest the following:

Brooks, J. G., & Brooks, M. G. (1993). *In search of understanding: The case for constructivist classrooms.* Alexandria, VA: Association for Supervision and Curriculum Development.

Ridley, D. S., McCombs, B., & Taylor, K. (1994). Walking the talk: Fostering self-regulated learning in the classroom. *Middle School Journal, 26*(2), 52–57.

goal three

Understanding and Implementing a
Student-Directed Approach to Discipline

Goal three is broken into several parts. First, we explain our view that under certain conditions, student self-discipline can be an effective reality in schools. Second, we discuss possible shortcomings of more traditional, teacher-directed forms of student discipline. Third, we explain the theoretical underpinnings of the La Cima Responsibility Plan, a realistic student-directed approach to discipline. This discussion is followed by a case study of how the plan was designed and implemented and a section on problems and positive results.

POSSIBILITIES FOR STUDENT SELF-DISCIPLINE

Do students have the capacity to regulate their own behavior in a classroom? We believe the answer is a conditional yes. The reservations that lead us to qualify our response do not lie with students; instead; they lie with educators. We think students can self-regulate their behavior if

1. teachers strive to create a positive classroom environment based on the learner-centered suggestions given earlier,

2. teachers and schools rethink their traditional philosophies about discipline and give students the opportunity to take responsibility for their own behaviors, and

3. teachers and schools demonstrate and take the time to teach students how to regulate their behavior.

Some teachers may not agree with us, so we have been careful to present a realistic view of this student-directed approach to discipline. We chronicled an on going application of this method in a middle school where one of the authors is employed as a teacher. Before describing our findings, however, we discuss shortcomings of more traditional forms of discipline.

SHORTCOMINGS OF TRADITIONAL FORMS OF DISCIPLINE

Traditional forms of discipline have many positive attributes. For example, Canter and Canter's (1976) model of assertive discipline, which is used in many schools, makes teachers aware of their rights, such as the right to teach without disruption or fear. Their method has helped many teachers who were intimidated by discipline problems to learn to be assertive instead of reactive and aggressive or avoidant and passive.

Another advantage of Canter and Canter's (1976) model of discipline is that the process of disciplining students does not take much time away from teaching. Names of misbehaving students and, if necessary, subsequent check marks are quickly and quietly written on the board. Students are immediately aware of the consequence of their misbehavior and thus are encouraged to refocus their attention to the task.

As is true of any model of discipline, the traditional, teacher-directed approaches also have their disadvantages. Based on the work of Jones (1987), Glenn (1990), and Nelson (1992), we offer three major shortcomings of more traditional forms of discipline. First, for some teachers, having to be the police, judge, and jury takes the fun out of teaching. Many teachers have carried the burden of being the authority in a "catch me if you can" environment. It is emotionally draining to attempt to facilitate a meaningful lesson when students are misbehaving. Most teachers do not enjoy being the "heavy." They would prefer to enjoy a lively and rewarding learning experience.

Teachers often do not feel they have a choice about being the disciplinarian. They feel it is their job to make sure that misbehaving students do not disrupt the learning of others. Most teachers have certainly felt peer and administrative pressure to be firm with students. In fact, many experienced educators tell new teachers that discipline is the key to being an effective teacher. A realistic question to ponder, however, is whether the teacher as sole authority for student behavior may actually contribute to some of their acting out. If students came to believe that they were equally responsible for managing their behavior and creating a rewarding learning experience, how might this impact the classroom environment and affect the teacher's burden as disciplinarian?

The second major shortcoming of more traditional forms of discipline is that teachers stop misbehavior but do not teach students to manage it. Teacher-directed forms of discipline typically are based on the notion that if students violate the rules, they immediately will be subjected to negative consequences. This is a very behavioral perspective in that there is little interest in why students violate the rules. We consider this to be short-term thinking. Teachers may win the battle (i.e., by immediately stopping the misbehavior), but they usually lose the war (i.e., students continue to misbehave over the weeks, months, years).

By not dealing with the thinking behind student misbehavior, teachers are inadvertently fostering several additional problems. Primarily, they are not getting closer to solving the root problem. Second, teachers are modeling that kids should just obey without problem solving for themselves. Ask if that is what you expect of yourself. Do you value being blindly subservient to powerful forces? Do you hold someone else responsible for managing your behavior? Teachers may believe that kids in middle or high school should have already learned to effectively manage their own behavior. Perhaps they should have, but many children haven't learned self-discipline.

The third major shortcoming of more traditional forms of discipline is the mistaken notion that the punisher, by making the violator suffer, can positively motivate violators to want to do better. Instead, in many cases, the results of making violators suffer are negative emotions and the desire to resist, get even, or to quit trying. None of these motives are likely to lead to positive learning experiences or to change. Ask yourself, if you were perceived to be behaving inappropriately by your superiors, what actions on their part would foster your motivation to explore openly and potentially change your behavior? Would you feel that your views on the situation should be heard and considered?

Nelson (1992) said that when teachers give up more traditional forms of discipline and begin to implement more student-directed ones, they should be prepared for a month of hell. It takes time for students and teachers to learn to trust and help each other. Most students and adults have been socialized to accept automatically the traditional, teacher-directed approaches to discipline as the norm. A shift to a model of discipline that is based on teaching students to be responsible is a strong departure from the norm. Learning to think and act in this new way takes time for everyone—including students, teachers, administrators, and parents. We now chronicle this learning process for a middle school in Arizona.

THE PRINCIPLES UNDERLYING A SCHOOLWIDE STUDENT SELF-DISCIPLINE PROGRAM

If the various approaches to classroom discipline could be conceptualized as points falling along a continuum with one end of the continuum being extreme teacher-directed approaches and the other end of the continuum being extreme student-directed approaches to discipline, the La Cima Responsibility Plan would lie closer the student-directed end, along with similar approaches by Thomas Gordon (1974, 1989), Rudolf Dreikurs and colleagues (Dreikurs & Cassel, 1972; Dreikurs, Greenwald, & Pepper, 1982) and William Glasser (1969, 1986). These student-directed approaches to discipline emphasize problem-solving, shared student–teacher power, reflective questioning, and remediation. On the other hand, La Cima Middle School's approach would be in sharp contrast to teacher-directed approaches by Lee Canter (Canter & Canter, 1976) and James Dobson (1970). These teacher-directed approaches to discipline emphasize rewards and conditioning, immediate and predetermined consequences, teacher power, physical intervention, and isolation.

Facilitators of the La Cima Responsibility Plan assume that students have the capacity to regulate their own learning and their behavior and assume that at all times students are trying to have one or more of their basic needs met (e.g., emotional safety, self-confidence, fun, belonging, power, freedom). When people choose accepted behaviors, they are able to meet their needs with a high degree of satisfaction from themselves and others. At other times, people may choose less accepted ways to satisfy their needs. Even though these less accepted behaviors may appear to be self-defeating or destructive to an outside observer, given how things look to individuals under certain circumstances, people do the best they can to choose behaviors that will meet their needs.

Beliefs about how people can get their needs met are shaped by past experiences and socialization. To the outside world, individuals have been well socialized if their beliefs about and means of need satisfaction match society's norms. Frequently, however, and for a variety of reasons, peoples' beliefs about and actions toward need satisfaction are viewed as unacceptable by society. For this reason, proponents of the La Cima project feel that it is necessary to structure educational experiences in ways that foster positive interactions with others so that students and adults can help each other develop successful prosocial, need-satisfying values and behaviors.

Within this framework, traditional punishment (e.g., detention) is no longer used because it (a) loses the remediating focus of replacing unacceptable need-satisfaction beliefs and behaviors with more prosocial ones, and (b) removes the responsibility for remediation from the misbehaving person and places it with someone or something else. The new plan focuses on teaching students responsibility for self-control through a problem-solving process approach.

The assumptions behind and purposes of this approach are supported by theory and research on self-regulated learning, especially the value placed on reflecting on one's choices and their consequences (e.g., Ridley, 1990, 1991; Ridley et al., 1994; Ridley, Schutz, Glanz, & Weinstein, 1992). Higher levels of reflection make it possible for one to assess his or her own thoughts, feelings, and behaviors. This reflection can impact, in a fundamental and profound way, "how things look" to an individual. It is this type of personal reflective experience that helps one to realize the limits of unacceptable beliefs and behaviors that have brought her or him suffering and problems of coping.

Higher levels of reflective awareness also increase consistency between intentions and actions. Reflectively intentional individuals typically have greater intention-to-action consistency because they are more aware of their purposes and act more consistently with their intentions (Ridley, 1990). On the other hand, individuals who are operating in an unreflective and automatic manner typically have lower intention-to-action consistency because they lack reflective clarity of their intentions. This lack of reflectivity makes some students vulnerable to becoming unpremeditated attention seekers in the classroom. The solution to these disruptive behaviors may not be externally administered punishment. Thus, many educators, including those at La Cima Middle School, are helping students to become more aware of and responsible for the appropriateness of their beliefs, choices, and behaviors for successfully coping in their environments.

CASE STUDY: LA CIMA MIDDLE SCHOOL

Several years ago, the teachers at the newly opened La Cima Middle School in the northwestern part of Tucson, Arizona, decided that the school's mission should be to foster the development of *independent learners*: that is, learners who are confident, motivated, and self-directed. After several years of a schoolwide effort to create instructional change to incorporate student-directed learning activities, the teachers at this school had not created a schoolwide discipline program. At the same time, the school was experiencing a range of discipline problems, most of them typical of many middle schools. Some of the problems, however, were more severe, and included drug sales and use, vandalism, and gang-related activities. Obviously, teachers and parents were greatly concerned. A group of the teachers campaigned for and convinced the others to adopt a hard-line approach, described by some teachers as the "witch hunt," where teachers sent students to the assistant principal for almost any violation. This approach was a very teacher-directed, "get-tough" means of responding to discipline problems.

During this difficult time at La Cima Middle School, a handful of teachers complained that the get-tough approach was inconsistent with their mission of creating independent learners. Contrary to the school's independent learner philosophy, teachers were setting policy and enacting punishment on the students. Students appeared to feel little responsibility or commitment to the rules. Discipline problems and referrals continued to grow to the point that the assistant principal was overwhelmed. In short, the get-tough approach was not working.

In time, others began to listen to the handful of teachers and administrators in the school who had advocated a student self-discipline approach that was consistent with the philosophy of creating independent learners. After reading books by Glasser (1986) and Jones (1987) about control theory and positive discipline, attending a workshop where Stephen Glenn spoke, and meeting with a consultant (Jim Fitzpatrick) about teaching students responsibility, a group of teachers, administrators, students, and parents at the school adapted a student self-discipline program that they called the La Cima Responsibility Plan. The program was presented to and approved by all faculty members.

In the following few sections, we describe the cornerstones of the La Cima Responsibility Plan: (a) the five levels of responsibility planning, (b) the eight principles for students' responsibility-planning success, and (c) the classroom meeting format. Teachers are reminded that these ideas don't have to be applied to every school in exactly the way they are presented here. Any program should be flexible enough to accommodate the needs and characteristics of each individual school. This case study serves as a chronicle of the ongoing evolution of this approach in a large city school with a diverse student population.

The Responsibility-Planning Process

The first cornerstone of the responsibility-planning approach to discipline is the use of student improvement plans for the development of alternative behaviors. La Cima Middle School has five levels of planning. These levels are progressive and are based on the frequency and seriousness of a student's discipline problems. The first level is called the quick fix. To use the *quick fix* a teacher asks a student, "What are you doing?" "What's the rule?" "Can you do that?" "Thank you!" Given that most discipline problems are minor classroom disturbances such as talking, the quick fix approach typically works quickly and quite well. For example, consider the following brief exchange:

EXAMPLE

Teacher:	Dionne, what are you doing?
Dionne:	Andrew is making faces at me!
Teacher:	Dionne, what are YOU doing?
Dionne:	I'm trying to write on Andrew's arm.
Teacher:	What's our rule?
Dionne:	Keep your hands to yourself.
Teacher:	Yes, dear, will you do that?
Dionne:	Yeah.
Teacher:	Thank you.

If after several opportunities this approach does not change the student's behavior, the next level may be applied. Verbal plans (level two) are an extension of the quick fix. Level two involves the same initial questions to students, but is followed by asking the student, "Is there anything you can do to make this right?" or "What else can you do next time this happens?" After the student gives a reasonable alternative plan—you may have to help them at first—you can thank the student and state, "I'm counting on you to do what you said." If you have to prompt the student to help him or her to create the alternative plan, it is important to make sure he or she understands how the plan will be beneficial. You might ask, "When this plan works, how will it improve life for you here at school?" For example, consider the following brief exchange:

Teacher: Dionne, what are you doing?

Dionne: I am hitting Andrew because he is messing with me.

Teacher: What is our rule?

Dionne: Keep your hands to yourself. But, he is LOOKING at me!

Teacher: Is hitting Andrew helping matters?

Dionne: No, but . . .

Teacher: Is there a way for you to solve this problem that doesn't violate our rules?

Dionne: [sullen] I don't know.

Teacher: How about sitting up here by Ashanti?

Dionne: Could I sit by the overhead?

Teacher: How would that help you solve your problem, Dionne?

Dionne: I wouldn't have to look at Andrew and I could pay attention.

Teacher: Great plan, Dionne.

In time, students like Dionne will learn to find solutions more quickly, independently, and ultimately more proactively. Time taken to patiently help students to establish this type of problem-solving-oriented thinking will pay dividends in the future.

It is suggested that you try a minimum of three verbal plans in your classroom before moving to the next planning level. At La Cima, level three consists of having the student work on a written plan in the classroom or in a buddy teacher's classroom (see Figure 1). At this level, logical or natural consequences are built into the plan. These consequences should be created by, or at least negotiated with, the student. The teacher helps the student with his or her plan, and should be supportive and respectful. The student stays in the teacher's or buddy teacher's classroom until the written plan is completed.

If after three attempts the plan is not successful, the planning process moves to the next level. At level four, the student is referred to the assistant principal's office (see Figure 2), who asks the student to work on a plan in the *planning room*. The planning room is not for punishment, so the environment of the room must be positive at all times. Students are asked to carefully think through their unsuccessful behaviors and to create a written plan to solve their problem situation (see Figure 3). Students stay in the planning room until they have completed their plan and approved it with the planning room monitor or the assistant principal. This level is for more severe infractions, for students who refuse to write a plan in a teacher's classroom, or for students who have experienced numerous planning failures for the same misbehaviors. At this level it is suggested that parents be notified.

For the few students who go to the next level of planning (five) by refusing to create or follow through on an alternative behavior plan, the policy at La Cima is to allow them a *decision day*. This is a session in which a plan is worked out by the principal, the parents, and the student that allows the student to continue to come to school on a day-by-day basis as long as no school rule is broken (see Figure 4). If a rule is broken, the parents agree to take the student home that day. Home-bound students must create a new plan and convince their parents and the principal of their commitment to the plan before they are allowed back into school.

Teachers at La Cima would want you to know that plans typically do not stop the misbehavior on the student's first try. Thus, teachers have to be patient. If the plan fails, it's time to replan. Also, teachers have to demonstrate a commitment to follow and reinforce the student's progress.

The Principles of Responsibility Planning

The second cornerstone of the La Cima Responsibility Plan approach to discipline are eight principles that serve as the basis for students' successful responsibility planning and implementation. The principles reported here are adapted from the work of Jim Fitzpatrick (1993), a school consultant who has contributed concrete suggestions to a number of schools interested in the application of a student self-discipline approach. Again, these principles are only guidelines and are not meant to be followed in an absolute or linear manner.

1. *Get students involved at all levels.* This means personal involvement among students and teachers. Personal involvement typically breeds commitment and respect. Teachers should take the time to get to know their students. They should use students' names and look for the positive aspects of each student. Teachers should also involve students in the planning and implementation of school improvement initiatives. Students can provide valuable insights to planning teams because their involvement can foster greater success. The other benefits of this involvement strategy are the same as those of strategies suggested earlier for meeting students' needs for emotional safety, self-confidence, and belonging.

2. *Deal with the present (not the past).* The purpose of a responsibility plan is to teach students new behaviors for the future. Past mistakes should not be relived or thrown up to students. To deal with the present, teachers should ask questions like, "What are you doing?" "What's going on?" Also, teachers should avoid asking questions like, "Why did you do that?" Many times students aren't able to express the "whys." They may lack reflectivity or act on impulse. The previous questions are designed to help students become more aware of the purposes for and consequences of their behaviors.

3. *Get the student to judge his or her own behavior.* Instead of passing judgment on violators' actions, ask questions that encourage them to judge their own behaviors. These questions might be, "Is your behavior in keeping with class rules?" "What's the rule?" "Can you do that?" "Is this behavior helping matters?" It may take time for students to adjust to this approach. These questions place the issue in the lap of the misbehaving student. At first, some students may try to blame others or change the subject. Stay focused and, if necessary, help the student accept ownership for the problem.

4. *Guide students to create plans for improving future behavior.* Ask the student to formulate an alternative way of behaving the next time he or she is confronted with a similar situation. As the five levels of responsibility planning demonstrate, the planning process should start small—one behavioral problem at a time. Monitor student plans to help ensure success. At the beginning, you may have to help some students by suggesting alternative behaviors because they honestly may not know what to do next time. The student plans with the greatest chance of success are short and conservative (i.e., have a 95% chance for success).

5. *Build students' commitment to their plans by giving them feedback and reinforcement.* Students will feel more committed if you acknowledge the validity of their plan. Doing this could be as simple as eye contact and a smile, or a pat on the back, or as complex as a scheduled meeting to discuss their plan and the consequences for success.

6. *Don't allow excuses.* Excuses serve only to pass on or avoid responsibility. Do not even entertain a discussion about excuses. Instead, ask students what they could do the next time they are confronted with a similar situation.

7. *Do not punish misbehaviors and failures to follow through on planned behaviors.* Punishment removes responsibility from the violator and shifts it to the punisher. This does not mean that planned consequences should be avoided. To the contrary, these consequences are a central part of students' behavioral plans, especially for more serious discipline problems. If students agree to certain consequences and fail to follow through on the alternative behaviors, they have made a conscious choice that commits them to their stated consequences.

8. *Give the responsibility-planning process time to work. (Don't give up.)* Teaching students to be responsible takes time even under the best circumstances. Many behaviors are a function of unconscious habits. As we all know, habits are hard to break. Fitzpatrick (1993) asked teachers to be patient once more than the student expects. This is difficult but excellent advice. Some students expect that teachers will give up on them. They may even work at it. Don't give up on students.

The Classroom Meeting

The last cornerstone of the responsibility-planning approach to discipline is the use of the classroom meeting. In his book *Schools Without Failure*, William Glasser (1969) suggested the use of class meetings as a way of teaching students to communicate, think about the various sides of an issue, and make decisions. Glasser envisioned that various agendas could be dealt with using the class meeting format, including social problem solving (i.e., dealing with student behavior issues), open-ended (i.e., dealing with any relevant student or teacher topic), and educational (i.e., dealing with issues related to student understanding of the curriculum). The following are a number of recommendations on the structure and facilitation of a class meeting.

1. *Have students sit in a large, tight circle arrangement.* To foster communication, all students need to be able to see and hear each other. Teachers know how easy it is for students in the back rows to "hide" from the discussion. The teacher should also rotate seats from one class meeting to another. For example, it may be wise at one time to sit beside a student who speaks too much. Another time, it may help to sit beside and encourage students who seldom speak.

2. *Consider the importance of timing.* Glasser also suggested that holding the meeting to a specific length every time is better than allowing the meeting length to vary from time to time. For middle and high school students, the average productive time for a class meeting is 30–50 minutes. Concerning frequency, Glasser stated that classroom meetings could be as frequent as daily. Given the demands of the curriculum, we suggest a once per week or bimonthly scheduling of class meetings, unless special circumstances call for an "emergency" class meeting.

3. *Subjects for the meetings may be introduced by the students or the teacher.* Part of the students' motivation to participate is the realization that all issues relevant to the class as a group or to any individual in the class are eligible for discussion. Strict censorship is likely to thwart the success of class meetings. On the other hand, to encourage feelings of safety, the teacher should guide students to develop rules for participation (e.g., listen respectfully, do not put other people down, whether present or not).

4. *To ensure understanding, have students define the topic to be discussed in their own words.* For example, if there has been a rash of student interruptions during class time, the class may choose to discuss this. To define the problem of interrupting, the teacher might ask students, "What is interrupting?" "What are different ways to interrupt?" "When is interruption good and bad?"

5. *To ensure that students perceive a topic's relevance, relate the topic to the students' world.* This breeds interest and involvement. The teacher might ask, "Do people ever interrupt you? How do you feel when this happens?" "Have you ever interrupted someone else? What happened? How did they feel? How did you feel?"

6. *To encourage thinking, ask questions that challenge students to come up with better ways of dealing with the topic area.* You might ask, "Is there a better way to interrupt someone? What should some of the class rules be about interrupting?"

7. *The teacher should not interrupt the student to correct grammar or mild profanity.* Given that the class meeting is designed to be an open forum, equally owned by all parties, corrective interruptions are often destructive to the discussions. This does not mean that the teacher should allow certain students to dominate the discussion. In this case, the teacher can suggest, "Let's hear from someone else; we'll come back to you if time permits."

8. *Class meetings to discuss behavioral problems should not focus on one student time after time.* Although there should be no reluctance to openly discuss individuals, the teacher should not allow the discussion to become destructive for or repetitive to a given student.

9. *Discussion of problems should be directed toward finding a solution.* Although the teacher needs to use his or her judgment to allow students to vent, problem-oriented class meetings should not just be "gripe sessions." After participants have had a chance to express their frustrations, gently encourage them to engage in constructive problem-solving steps.

We suggest that class meetings end with a brief evaluation of how it went. This allows students greater ownership of the outcome and gives the facilitator valuable suggestions about how to improve the meetings. Teachers may be surprised by how effective these meetings can be to discuss and solve previously "unsolvable" classroom problems. The reports from and experiences of teachers at La Cima Middle School indicated that students like to discuss and make choices about themselves.

Teachers at La Cima Middle School have observed that students at this age have insight and, when they learn how to communicate and to make decisions, they are able to solve almost any problem. Teachers state that students must know that they are respected and believed in to be willing to open up and be "real" with you. Consistency and clear, honest, and nonpatronizing communication are also very important to success.

Reflections on the Responsibility-Planning Process

According to the teachers, when the Responsibility Plan was first introduced to the students, the responsibility-planning process went surprisingly well. Students were, however, a bit taken aback when they were asked to create improvement plans of action for their misbehaviors. Previously at La Cima—during the "witch hunt"—students were more used to having punishment handed down to them. Students seemed to adjust to the responsibility plan more quickly than many teachers expected, although they say that they find the process of writing improvement plans to be a difficult chore. Students say this is especially true when teachers expect quality plans from them. Having high expectations means that students are expected to sit down and really reflect on their misbehavior and to create and implement thoughtful alternative behaviors.

Another teacher observation is that the students who are in greatest need for responsibility-planning interventions are the recent transfers to the school. Some teachers have concluded that these students are more accustomed to being told what to do and how to do it, and given consequences than they are to managing their own behavior. Teachers report that these students are slower to adapt to the responsibility-planning system; in fact, some of them push the limits to see if the system is for real. Fortunately, most of the teachers at La Cima stayed firm to the philosophy of the responsibility plan and have been willing to go the extra mile to teach these kids how to succeed with self-management.

Perhaps the two greatest tests for the responsibility plan have been the loss of the administrator who was in charge overseeing the entire Responsibility Plan program at La Cima and teacher inconsistency in implementing the new system. When the assistant principal was promoted, she was replaced by a person who was new to administration. This new administrator had the huge task of learning the ropes of a new job that included managing the Responsibility Plan. This change, as well as philosophical differences among some of the existing faculty, has brought about some inconsistencies in how students' cases were managed.

Not all individuals fully understand the "big picture" of the Responsibility Plan, nor do all faculty and staff fully believe in it. Some of the teachers at the school who are oriented more toward traditional forms of discipline feel they don't have enough time to deal with plans. Some of these teachers still tend to present the improvement planning process to students as punishment (i.e., "You better get your act together NOW or you will have to write a plan!"). In these classrooms, some students have reacted with disruption, most likely, to test the genuineness of the Responsibility Plan concept.

To manage these difficulties, the insights of teachers with differing views are considered for the insight they can provide to strengthening the Responsibility Plan. Additionally, during hiring interviews, teacher applicants are asked certain questions in an attempt to determine if their philosophical views are similar to those in La Cima's vision and mission. In spite of the slumps, backsteps, mistakes, and challenges since 1992, the La Cima Responsibility Plan has survived and grown. It has become a priority program and has been written into the school's strategic plan. Faculty and staff meet regularly for inservice and staff development meetings during which people are encouraged to vent their frustrations and share their successes.

The teachers report that one reason the Responsibility Plan has been a success is that the faculty and staff planned for change and even welcomed it. They have also demonstrated a constancy of purpose (i.e., to eliminate punishment and coercion and to place the responsibility of self-regulation on the student) and an ongoing willingness to communicate and learn. This flexible planning, commitment, and open communication have translated into improved student behavior. From 1992 to the end of 1994 the assistant principal's office calculated the following figures:

❑ Campus/classroom disruptions have decreased 35%.

❑ Unexcused absences have decreased 56%.

❑ Excessive tardies have decreased 71%.

❑ Vandalism/theft/arson has decreased 50%.

❑ Weapons/prohibited objects have decreased 37%.

❑ Bus referrals have decreased 20%.

Again, although acknowledging the success of teacher-directed approaches to discipline in some schools, we believe that educators who value and espouse the mission of fostering the development of independent or self-regulated learners should logically be drawn to the more student-directed approaches to discipline like the La Cima Responsibility Plan. This school community believes that student behavior (i.e., the development of more effective prosocial skills) is an aspect of the overall educational experience inseparable from more traditionally conceived academic learning.

1. Where would you say your beliefs about effective discipline fall along the student-directed to teacher-directed continuum?

2. What experiences shape your beliefs about effective discipline?

3. What aspects of the student-directed approaches to discipline appeal to you most?

4 How much do you think your students would say you teach or foster responsibility in the classroom?

5 What is one thing you could change in your classroom to better teach and foster responsibility?

6 How will you measure whether your idea(s) is (are) effective (e.g., What indicators will you look for?)?

1 As you know, when students misbehave and make bad choices in class, different teachers will do different things. One teacher might quickly give the misbehaving student a consequence like a referral, a detention, and so on, and keep on teaching. Another teacher might stop teaching for a moment and have the misbehaving student think about how he or she could make a better decision next time. The first teacher's main concern is trying to stop the student's misbehavior because it is interfering with the lesson. The second teacher's main concern is teaching the misbehaving student how to behave more responsibly. If you were the teacher, what would be your main concern? Explain why.

(Remind everyone of the rules the group has created for participation, such as, listen respectfully, no put-downs, etc.)

1. What is (are) the issue(s) for this meeting? Make the issue clear by having everyone

   ☐ put the issue into their own words.

   ☐ talk about how they feel about the issue.

   ☐ explain how the issue affects them.

2. What is the desired change (if applicable)? Make the desired change clear by having everyone say

   ☐ what they would like to see happen.

   ☐ what they are willing to do differently.

   ☐ when the change will be carried out.

   ☐ who is responsible for carrying out the change.

   ☐ how they will reinforce the success of the idea(s).

How was the meeting successful? What could be done next time to make the meeting more effective?

ADDITIONAL READING

For further reading about the Responsibility Planning process and about the use of classroom meetings we suggest the following:

Fitzpatrick, J. (1993). *Developing responsible behavior in schools.* South Burlington, VT: Fitzpatrick Associates.

Glasser, W. (1969). *Schools without failure.* New York: Harper & Row.

Glasser, W. (1986). *Control theory in the classroom.* New York: Harper & Row.

FIGURE 1	**LA CIMA MIDDLE SCHOOL – MY PLAN**

"I am responsible for my actions and behavior."
"I will do what I say I will do."

Name _____ Grade _____ Date _____

WHEN WRITING YOUR PLAN:

1. Words like "try, never, always, rest of the year/etc." are not acceptable if included in your plan.
2. "Making excuses" for your behavior is unacceptable. You are responsible for your behavior—no one else!
3. Your answers need to be detailed, thoughtful, and in complete sentences. This means one-word answers are not acceptable.

I was referred to the office because …

_____

This referral could have been prevented if …

_____

In the future my attitude and behavior will be more responsible because I will …

_____

MY RESPONSIBILITY AND IMPROVEMENT PLAN:

(Include what you "need" to help you be successful.)

_____

_____

_____

I will follow through with my **PLAN** from now until _____ / _____ / _____
when I check-in with _____

In order to make my **PLAN** work, I need to make sure I … _____

_____

Student Signature _____ Date _____
Student made **PLAN** with_____ Date _____
Checked-in: _____YES _____ NO
Student meeting **PLAN** expectations: _____YES _____ NO
Parent Signature (if present) _____ Date _____

FIGURE 2	**LA CIMA MIDDLE SCHOOL – OFFICE REFERRAL**

Student Name _____ **Grade** _____ **Date** _____
Referral made by _____

REASON FOR DISCIPLINARY REFERRAL:

_____ 01 Disruption - Campus

_____ 02 Disruption - Classroom

_____ 04 Assault

_____ 05 Weapons

_____ 06 Dangerous/Prohibited Objects

_____ 07 Theft

_____ 09 Prohibited Drugs

_____ 19 Arson

_____ 31 Unexcused Absence

_____ 32 Excessive Tardies

_____ 35 Fighting

_____ 50 Violated Verbal Plan

_____ 51 Violated Written Plan

_____ 52 Violated Verbal/Written Plan

_____ 41 Other School Policies (explanation below)

STEPS TAKEN PRIOR TO REFERRAL:

_____ Verbal Plan(s)

_____ Written Plan(s)

_____ Counselor Referral

_____ Parent Contact

_____ Additional Information

_____

_____

_____

_____

_____

_____

_____

_____

_____

_____

COMMENTS:

_____

_____

_____

ADMINISTRATIVE ACTION TAKEN:

_____ Pupil Verbally Corrected

_____ Planning Room Assigned

_____ Office Verbal Plan

_____ Office Written Plan

_____ Decision Day

_____ Out-of-School Suspension Assigned/Dates _____

_____ Counselor Referral

_____ Parent Contact

_____ Student/Family Advocate

_____ Police Contact

COMMENTS:

_____

_____

Administrative Signature _____ Date _____

FIGURE 3	STUDENT RESPONSE PACKET № 5.1

Disrupted class (1) _____ Name _____

Date _____

Grade _____ Homeroom _____

INTRODUCTION

These pages are designed to help you apply some of the information in the Learning Packet to your own situation. The purpose of the response form is to improve your understanding of why you disturbed a class and to help you avoid further problems of a similar nature by looking at your own behavior and setting goals for yourself.

QUESTIONS

Answer each in the space provided. If more room is needed you may use the back of the page. Make certain your answers are in complete sentences. Proper grammar and correct spelling are expected. When you finish, turn in the packet to the detention supervisor and return to your desk to await dismissal.

1. What class did you disturb?

2. Who is the teacher?

3. Describe what the class was doing (or supposed to be doing) just before you decided to disturb the class.

FIGURE 3 (CONT'D)

4. Describe exactly what you did to disturb the class.

5. Explain why you disturbed this particular class.

6. Have you had similar problems in this class? If yes, explain what happened previously.

7. Have you had similar problems in any other class? If yes, explain what happened.

8. How did the teacher attempt to discipline you this time for being a disturbance? About how much time did the teacher spend trying to correct the situation?

9. What should you have been doing instead of misbehaving?

10. Which of the three types of class disruptions described in the Learning Packet[1] is most similar to the one you caused? Why?

11. Explain what you could have done to prevent this class disruption.

12. List three specific steps you could take to improve your disruptive tendencies.

a.

b.

c.

[1]The three types of class disruptions are (a) outburst and frustration, (b) bored or attention-getting, and (c) reacting behavior. The Learning Packet is an introduction to the student response plan. It describes reasons why students choose inappropriate actions to meet their needs and suggests alternative ways to think about misbehavior.

FIGURE 4	**LA CIMA MIDDLE SCHOOL – DECISION DAY REFERRAL**

Each student at La Cima Middle School is treated as a distinct individual with unique needs when rules and expectations are applied. He or she has the opportunity to develop individual "Responsibility Plans." When a student has not taken advantage of this opportunity to be responsible for his or her own actions, La Cima Middle School strongly supports removing the student to his or her home to facilitate the student being able to make responsible decisions about his or her own behavior.

Name of Student _____

Date _____ **Grade** _____ **Team** _____

STEPS TAKEN PRIOR TO THIS OPTION:

_____ Verbal Plan(s) _____ Written Plan(s) _____ Planning Room Assignment

COMMENTS:

_____

_____

_____

Student Signature _____ Date _____
Administrative Signature _____ Date _____
Parent/Guardian Signature _____ Date _____

Student was removed to the home at _____

Date student may return to school: _____

PARENTS/GUARDIANS MUST ACCOMPANY THE STUDENT WHEN HE OR SHE RETURNS TO THE LA CIMA MIDDLE SCHOOL CAMPUS. Please call the office to schedule a conference with the assistant principal.

goal four

Understanding the Limits and Obstacles to
Implementing These Recommendations

In goal four, we discuss some of the teacher- and school-level barriers that must be overcome to successfully implement the strategies presented in this book. We are confident that all the suggestions in this book can be successfully implemented. The research we have cited is testimony to this, but possibly even more convincing to some teachers is that we and other teachers we know are currently using many of these methods with success.

To be objective, we must point out that building a positive classroom environment—one that meets the needs of students and fosters student self-discipline—does place strong demands on teachers and administrators. A review of goal two, for instance, should convince the reader that meeting students' six basic affective/motivational needs takes a lot of time. The same is true for teaching responsibility. You must take the time to develop verbal and written plans for future behavior. You must be willing to meet with your students and evaluate the effectiveness of their plans. You must, at times, be painfully patient with students who struggle to change their dysfunctional behaviors.

To complicate matters, there often aren't enough school personnel to serve as planning supervisors (e.g., in the planning room), and there always seem to be scheduling problems (e.g., How much time can I allow for class meetings this week?), and unexpected events that obstruct the routine. Below are some of the limits and obstacles that must be managed to successfully implement the strategies presented in this book.

1. *Time.* Time is always a factor in public education. School staff never seem to have enough of it. The bottom line is that teachers and administrators have to ask themselves if positive classroom environments and student self-discipline skills are important enough priorities to take the time to foster. We think so. Although meeting students' needs and developing responsible behaviors in schools takes a lot of time, fortunately, after the strategies are implemented, they can actually save time.

2. *Teachers' different views about their roles.* In most schools one will find varied philosophies on education and discipline. Some teachers at the middle school we have been reporting on still believe that discipline is the responsibility of the office. If you looked into each classroom at this school, you would find varying degrees of teacher commitment to the La Cima Responsibility Plan. Strong differences in teacher beliefs can create an image of inconsistency for students (e.g., some teachers have

their students figure out their own problem behaviors along with suitable alternatives, whereas others are still more oriented toward telling their students what to do). We believe that to a degree this type of variance in teacher beliefs is inevitable. Teachers, like everyone else, have different personalities and beliefs. Any successful school-wide approach to instruction or discipline has to plan for this.

3. *The school's willingness to commit resources to make new instructional approaches or discipline programs successful.* Teachers do need support. Staff development and in-service training are needed to provide constancy of purpose. Training is also needed to develop new attitudes, skills, and techniques, including problem solving and shared decision making. Administrators must be willing to give teachers more control over staff development and decision making, and they must allow teachers to experiment if these learner-centered recommendations are to be successful.

4. *Willingness to share classroom control.* Sharing control in the classroom is an important and personal issue that deserves more extensive discussion here. This issue relates to how confident and comfortable you are as a teacher in sharing the control of learning activities with your students. The research of Ashton and Webb (1986), Woolfolk and Hoy (1990), and many others on teacher self-efficacy has demonstrated that teachers who question their own ability to get through to students (i.e., have lower teaching efficacy) are less likely to share classroom control. Instead, these teachers use instructional techniques oriented toward containment and control (e.g., one-way lecture, drill and individual practice, little or no self-disclosures, manipulative praise, little time allowed for independent work, few student choices, little or no group activities). If group activities are directed by controlling teachers, low-achieving students are frequently grouped together and receive less attention than higher achieving students.

Not only does this excessive control by teachers make the learning environment less positive and offer few opportunities for self-discipline, research also indicates that it leads students to think and act as if they are not capable of more autonomous learning.

Specifically, Grolnick and Ryan (1989) found that not only do students in a heavily controlled learning environment act more like "pawns" (i.e., they are dependent, passively compliant, reactive, or rebellious), they may reciprocally pull teachers into being even more controlling. Research by Deci and Ryan (1987) has also established that teachers' overcontrolling behaviors reduce students' achievement. These researchers believed that greater teacher control reduces students' feelings of self-determination, intrinsic motivation, and performance.

Why might teachers be unwilling to share the control of learning activities with their students? One possible reason is suggested by the work of Flink et al. (1990). This research suggests that administrative pressure on teachers to demonstrate high student performance, as measured by achievement tests (versus fostering the learning process) promotes teachers' controlling behaviors. Also, given the negative media-induced image of the American educational system, many teachers feel the pressure to "produce." Some teachers bend to this pressure and teach to the test, but in many cases scores still decline. The research of Flink et al. suggests that this pressure to produce students with high test scores has a cost of lowering teacher effectiveness, creating a more negative learning environment, and lowering levels of student learning.

In summary, in school environments where test-score accountability is extremely high, curricula and school policy are dictated in a top-down manner, classroom sizes are growing, time and in-service training resources are limited, and teacher confidence is low, we are concerned about the challenges individuals face when attempting to incorporate these recommendations. The research suggests that the teachers who are most likely to carry out these recommendations are the ones who perceive their schools as places that foster teacher autonomy, risk-taking, and ongoing personal and professional development. Ryan and Stiller (1991) concluded that "the capacity of teachers to promote self-regulation and internalization of value for learning in students is inexorably intertwined with teachers' opportunities to regulate their own activities and thus to be innovative, creative, and intrinsically motivated on a day-to-day basis (p.23)."

Thus, researchers (e.g., Glasser, 1986; Ryan & Stiller, 1991) suggest what many teachers already know. For teachers to be able to value and strive to meet students' basic needs, those responsible for managing teachers' working environments must also value and strive to meet teachers' needs. We suggest that building administrators heed this advice and consider ways of adapting the strategies in this book for their teachers.

Ultimately, the responsibility for creating a positive learning environment is a collective one shared by a number of people: students, teachers, building and central administrators, parents, and society in general. We believe that this responsibility is shared in a cyclical manner. As with a chain, the weakest link will determine the overall level of success. Thus, teachers and administrators must promote safety, confidence, fun, belonging, respect, interpersonal warmth, choice and responsibility, reflectivity, risk-taking, and learning for its own sake. Schools must also aggressively seek the support of parents and community members who value these virtues because school staff members, by themselves, do not have all the ideas or the resources needed to ensure the success of all students.

We know that the kind of positive changes that we have presented in this book can happen in real schools. We have experienced it and continue to strive for it. If you look around—you probably won't have to look far— you, too, will find teachers and schools that are achieving positive changes every day. Even with all the obstacles, limits, bumps, and setbacks these educators succeed because they truly want to create places of responsibility and meaningful learning.

1 How much do you think your school environment fosters or limits the implementation of recommendations like those presented in this book?

2 What is one thing you could change in your school environment to foster the implementation of these recommendations?

3 Who else in your school and in your community would be committed to helping you foster the implementation of these recommendations?

Final Review

This book has provided a perspective on the nature of a positive classroom environment and of student self-discipline. The information and suggestions are based on classroom research and experience suggesting that teachers are best able to achieve these goals when they strive to meet student needs.

□ Goal 1: Defining a Positive Classroom Environment

We point out that there are two major differences in the nature of the factors that students and teachers use to define a positive classroom environment. First, students define a positive classroom environment by using factors that are much more personal and affective than those used by teachers. Second, both students and teachers have a need for a sense of personal control over the direction of the learning experience. However, this common need often leads to more student–teacher conflict than consensus. These two major differences are the focal point of our argument that teachers are best able to create a positive classroom environment when they acknowledge and strive to satisfy students' affective/motivational needs.

□ Goal 2: Meeting Students' Needs for a Positive Classroom Environment

We suggested that if teachers are to be successful in fostering meaningful learning, they must strive to meet students' affective/motivational needs. We think that the consequences of the teachers' efforts to meet these needs are clear and direct: Students will be meaningfully engaged in the learning process. We discuss six basic affective/motivational needs of students (i.e., emotional safety, self-confidence, fun, belonging, power, freedom) and offer a number of teaching strategies for meeting these needs.

□ Goal 3: Understanding and Implementing a Student-Directed Approach to Discipline

We address the question of students' capacity to regulate their own behavior in a classroom. We believe in students' behavioral self-regulation abilities, but our belief is conditional. The reservations that lead us to qualify our response focus on educators. We think students can self-regulate their behavior if (a) teachers strive to create a positive classroom environment (based on the learner-centered suggestion given earlier), (b) teachers and other school personnel rethink their traditional philosophies about discipline and give students the opportunity to take responsibility for their own behaviors, and (c) teachers and schools take the time to teach students how to self-regulate their behavior.

We also present some of the possible shortcomings of traditional, teacher-directed forms of discipline. Finally, we present a case study of La Cima Middle School in Tucson, Arizona, that chronicled the ongoing evolution of a student-directed approach to discipline in a large city school with a diverse student population.

The cornerstones of the La Cima Responsibility Plan are (a) the responsibility planning process, (b) the principles for responsibility planning, and (c) the classroom meeting. Teachers are reminded that the ideas don't have to be applied to every school in an absolute manner. In fact, a large part of the success of the La Cima Responsibility Plan is based on the fact that La Cima staff has allowed for flexibility and change. Since 1992, this approach has led to significant reductions in a number of discipline problems at La Cima Middle School.

□ Goal 4: Understanding the Limits and Obstacles to Implementing These Recommendations

If teachers are to be able to foster positive learning experiences for their students, the school in which they work must also provide teachers the same positive opportunity. This opportunity comes through broad and open communication, consensus, and committed action for the purpose of reaching these goals.

Glossary

Academic impact—the influence of an intervention on a student's deep-level understanding and grade achievement (i.e., performance).

Classroom environment—the physical setting chosen for the facilitation of learning and the complex interdependent dynamics within that context. The classroom environment has various dimensions including social, cultural, personal, political, physical, economic, organizational, developmental, emotional, moral, religious, and psychological. The processes of communicating and developing new intrapersonal and interpersonal understandings across these numerous interwoven dimensions are the primary occurrences within the classroom environment.

Control theory—a theory of action based on the notion that behavior is goal directed.

Failure-avoiding strategies (face-saving strategies)—student behaviors, usually self-defeating, that are designed to avoid the vulnerability inherent in learning experiences. Predominant in performance-oriented classrooms, these behaviors trade off academic learning for the protection of one's self-image and self-esteem.

Goal-setting and shaping—a teaching strategy for increasing the academic confidence of students. Goal-setting should involve a consensus between student and teacher on a meaningful target outcome. Shaping is the use of a series of tasks involving small, graduated increases in task complexity until the target outcome is reached. The teacher must positively reinforce student effort and also student success at each step.

La Cima Responsibility Plan—a schoolwide approach to discipline based on the notion that teachers must help students learn to be more responsible and to make effective choices.

Learner-centered orientation—a perspective that takes the learner's unique frame of reference into account in designing, implementing, and assessing educational experiences. The goal is to understand how the learner perceives and values the learning experience and to strive to meet learners' needs in the learning process.

Mastery grading—a learning and assessment process that allows students to resubmit work for a higher grade in order to master their understanding of the task or concept.

Meaningful learning—the achievement of a deeper level of understanding in which information is transferred from an abstract academic concept to useful information applicable to one's broader personal life.

Motivational state—the individual's judgments and intentions related to a given task.

Personal context—a setting where simple acceptance and respect for fellow human beings is prioritized above any other role, goal, or outcome.

Proactive learning strategies—learning behaviors that lead to student success (e.g., effective note-taking, listening skills, comprehension monitoring skills, questioning skills, help-seeking behaviors, stress-management skills).

Process view of learning—the belief and practice of learning as a process instead of a contest. A focus on the joy of learning for its own sake. A commitment to effort as the key to success in learning.

Product view of learning—a contest-oriented view of learning that stresses comparative achievement. A focus on grade achievement as the primary motivation for learning. Ability is the key to successful learning.

Prosocial need-satisfying behaviors—need-satisfying behaviors that do not have a negative consequence on others. Prosocial skills may also include behaviors that create mutually satisfying outcomes.

Self-regulated learning—the process of interpreting, planning, and behaving within a given learning experience. Self-regulated learning varies on a continuum from habitual (i.e., unreflectively automatic self-regulation) to purposeful (i.e., reflectively intentional self-regulation). Reflectively intentional self-regulated learning is fostered through greater reflective self-awareness.

Student affective/motivational needs—basic emotional needs that determine whether the learner wants to or feels able to engage in the learning activity. These needs are emotional safety, self-confidence, fun, belonging, power, and freedom.

Student self-discipline—an approach to discipline that stresses learning to take responsibility for one's choices as opposed to teacher reward or punishment.

Student-led learning activities—learning activities that are implemented mainly by students with the indirect facilitation of the teacher. These activities could also be planned jointly among students and teacher. Possible examples include student projects, demonstrations, discussions, debates, role-plays, student mini-teaches, and other cooperative learning activities.

Teacher-centered orientation—a traditional behavioral view of teaching and learning in which the teacher bases instructional and professional responsibility decisions on a classroom frame of reference instead of an individual-student frame of reference.

References

Ames, C. (1992). Classrooms: Goals, structures, and student motivation. *Journal of Educational Psychology, 84*(3), 261–271.

Ashton, P. T., & Webb, R. B. (1986). *Making a difference: Teachers' sense of efficacy and student achievement.* New York: Longman.

Bandura, A. (1986). *Social foundations of thought and action: A social cognitive theory.* Englewood Cliffs, NJ: Prentice Hall.

Bangert-Drowns, R. L., Kulik, C. C., Kulik, J. A., & Morgan, M. (1991). The instructional effects of feedback in test-like events. *Review of Educational Research, 61,* 213–238.

Brekelmans, M., Wubbels, T., & Levy, J. (1993). Student performance, attitudes, instructional strategies, and teacher-communication style. In T. Wubbels & J. Levy (Eds.), *Do you know what you look like? Interpersonal relationships in education (56–63)*. Washington, DC: Falmer Press.

Brooks, J. G., & Brooks, M. G. (1993). *In search of understanding: The case for constructivist classrooms.* Alexandria, VA: Association for Supervision and Curriculum Development Publications.

Brophy, J. (1987). Synthesis of research on strategies for motivating students to learn. *Educational Leadership, 45(2),* 40–48.

Burke, J. (1991). Teenagers, clothes, and gang violence. *Educational Leadership, 49(1),* 11–14.

Calabrese, R. L. (1989). Student alienation and academic achievement. *Education Digest, 54(9),* 7–9.

Callen-Stoiber, K. C. (1991). The effect of technical and reflective preservice instruction on pedagogical reasoning and problem-solving. *Journal of Teacher Education, 42(2),* 131–139.

Canter, L., & Canter, M. (1976). *Assertive discipline: A take charge approach for today's educator.* Seal Beach, CA: Cantor and Associates.

Catterall, J. S. (1986). An intensive group counseling dropout prevention intervention: Some cautions on isolating at-risk adolescents within high school. *American Educational Research Journal, 24,* 521–540.

Collins, A., Brown, J. S., & Newman, S. E. (1989). Cognitive apprenticeship: Teaching the crafts of reading, writing, and mathematics. In L. B. Resnick (Ed.), *Knowing, learning, and instruction: Essays in honor of Robert Glaser (453–494)*. Hillsdale, NJ: Erlbaum.

Covington, M. V. (1992). *Making the grade: A self-worth perspective on motivation and school reform.* New York: Cambridge University Press.

Crain, R. L., Mahard, R. E., & Norot, R. E. (1989). *Making desegregation work.* Cambridge, MA: Ballinger.

deCharms, R. (1983). Intrinsic motivation, peer tutoring, and cooperative learning: Practical maxims. In J. Levine & M. Wang (Eds.), *Teacher and student perceptions: Implications for learning (391–398).* Hillsdale, NJ: Erlbaum.

Deci, E. L., & Ryan, R. M. (1985). *Intrinsic motivation and self-determination in human behavior.* New York: Plenum.

Deci, E. L., & Ryan, R. M. (1987). The support of autonomy and the control of behavior. *Journal of Personality and Social Psychology, 53,* 1024–1037.

Dobson, J. (1970). *Dare to discipline.* Wheaton, IL: Tyndale House.

Dreikurs, R., & Cassel, P. (1972). *Discipline without tears.* New York: Hawthorn Books.

Dreikurs, R., Grunwald, B., & Pepper, F. (1982). *Maintaining sanity in the classroom: Classroom management techniques* (2nd ed.). New York: Harper & Row.

Dweck, C. S. (1986). Motivational processes affecting learning. *American Psychologist, 41,* 1040–1048.

Edmonds, R. (1986). Characteristics of effective schools. In U. Neisser (Ed.), *The school achievement of minority children (93–104).* Hillsdale, NJ: Erlbaum.

Emmer, E. T., Evertson, C., Clements, B., & Worsham, M. (1994). *Classroom management for secondary teachers* (3rd ed.). Boston: Allyn & Bacon.

Fine, M. (1986). Why urban adolescents drop into and out of public high school. *Teachers College Record, 87,* 393–409.

Finn, J. (1989). Withdrawing from school. *Review of Educational Research, 59,* 117–142.

Finn, J. (1992, April). *Participation among 8th grade students at risk.* Paper presented at the annual meeting of the American Educational Research Association, San Francisco.

Fitzpatrick, J. (1993). *Developing responsible behavior in schools.* South Burlington, VT: Fitzpatrick Associates.

Flink, C., Boggiano, A. K., & Barrett, M. (1990). Controlling teaching strategies: Undermining children's self-determination and performance. *Journal of Personality and Social Psychology, 59*(5), 916–924.

Fordham, S., & Ogbu, J. (1986). Black students' school success: Coping with the burden of acting white. *Urban Review, 18,* 176–206.

Gardner, H. (1991). *The unschooled mind: How children think and how schools should teach.* New York: Basic Books.

Glasser, W. (1969). *Schools without failure.* New York: Harper & Row.

Glasser, W. (1986). *Control theory in the classroom.* New York: Harper & Row.

Glenn, S. (1990). *Raising self-reliant children in a self-indulgent world.* Rockland, CA: Prima.

Goodenow, C., & Grady, K. E. (1993). The relationship of school belonging and friends' values. *Journal of Experimental Education, 62*(1), 60–71.

Gordon, T. (1974). *Teacher effectiveness training.* New York: David McKay.

Gordon, T. (1989). *Teaching children self-discipline.* New York: Random House.

Grolnick, W. S., & Ryan, R. M. (1989). Parent styles associated with children's self-regulation and competence in school. *Journal of Educational Psychology, 81,* 143–154.

Holt, J. (1970). *What do I do on Monday?* New York: Dutton.

Hunter, M. (1991). Hunter design helps achieve the goals of science instruction. *Educational Leadership, 48*(4), 79–81.

Johnson, D. W., & Johnson, R. T. (1991). *Learning together and alone: Cooperative, competitive, and individualistic learning* (3rd ed.). Boston: Allyn & Bacon.

Jones, F. (1987). *Positive classroom discipline.* New York: McGraw-Hill.

Kagan, D. M. (1990). How schools alienate students at risk: A model for examining proximal classroom variables. *Educational Psychologist, 25*(2), 105–125.

Kehoe-Schwartz, E., Scott, V., & Birman, B. F. (1994). Student mobility in the nation's elementary schools. *Educational Considerations, 22*(1), 13–19.

King, N. J., Gullone, E., & Dadds, M. R. (1990). Student perceptions of permissiveness and teacher-instigated disciplinary strategies. *British Journal of Educational Psychology, 60,* 322–329.

Maslow, A. H. (1970). *Motivation and personality* (2nd ed.). New York: Harper & Row.

McCombs, B. L. (1993). Strategies for assessing and enhancing motivation: Keys to promoting self-regulated learning and performance. In H. F. O'Neil, Jr. & M. Drillings (Eds.), *Motivation: Research and theory* (pp. 49–69). Hillsdale, NJ: Erlbaum.

Midgely, C. (1991). Teacher sense of efficacy and the transition to middle level schools. *Middle School Journal, 22(5)*, 10–14.

Morgan, M. (1985). Self-monitoring of attained subgoals in private study. *Journal of Educational Psychology, 77,* 623–630.

Nelson, J. (1992). *Positive discipline in the classroom.* Rockland, CA: Prima.

Nuthall, G., & Alton-Lee, A. (1990). Research on teaching and learning: Thirty years of change. *Elementary School Journal, 90,* 540–570.

Oldfather, P. (1992, April). *My body feels completely wrong: Students' experiences when lacking motivation for academic tasks.* Paper presented at the annual meeting of the American Educational Research Association, San Francisco.

Oldfather, P. (1993). What students say about motivating experiences in a whole language classroom. *Reading Teacher, 46(8),* 672–681.

Ovadia, A. (1994). Reasoning patterns inhibiting school effectiveness: The case of the fallacy of bifurcation. *Urban Review, 26(1),* 35–40.

Prawat, R. S. (1992). Teachers' beliefs about teaching and learning: A constructivist perspective. *American Journal of Education, 100,* 354–395.

Richards, M. (1987). A teacher's action research study: The "bums" of 8H. *Peabody Journal of Education, 64(3),* 65–79.

Ridley, D. S. (1990). *Reflective intentionality: The development of a model of purposeful self-regulation*. Unpublished doctoral dissertation, University of Texas at Austin.

Ridley, D. S. (1991). Reflective self-awareness: A basic motivational process. *Journal of Experimental Education, 60*(1), 31–48.

Ridley, D. S., McCombs, B. L., & Taylor, K. D. (1994). Walking the talk: Fostering self-regulated learning in the classroom. *Middle School Journal, 26*(2), 52–57.

Ridley, D. S., Schutz, P. A., Glanz, R. S., & Weinstein, C. E. (1992). Self-regulated learning: The interactive influence of metacognitive awareness and goal-setting. *Journal of Experimental Education, 60*(4), 293–306.

Rosenthal, R., & Jacobson, L. (1968). *Pygmalion in the classroom: Teacher expectations and pupil's intellectual development*. New York: Holt, Rinehart & Winston.

Ryan, R. M. (1991). The nature of the self in autonomy and relatedness. In G. R. Goethals & J. Strauss (Eds.), *Multidisciplinary perspectives on the self*. New York: Springer-Verlag.

Ryan, R. M., & Stiller, J. (1991, April). *The social contexts of internalization: Parent and teacher influences on autonomy, motivation and learning*. Paper presented at the annual meeting of the American Educational Research Association, Chicago.

Schlosser, L. K. (1992). Teacher distance and student disengagement: School lives on the margin. *Journal of Teacher Education, 43*(2), 128–140.

Schuler, D. B. (1990). Effects of family mobility on student achievement. *ERS Spectrum, 6*(4), 17–24.

Schunk, D. H. (1991). Goal-setting and self-evaluation: A social cognitive perspective on self-regulation. In M. L. Maehr & P. R. Pintrich (Eds.), *Advances in motivation and achievement* (Vol. 7) (85–113). Greenwich, CT: JAI Press.

Shoop, R. (1990). A free student press fosters student responsibility. *Educational Leadership, 48*(3), 69–72.

Wehlage, G. C., & Rutter, R. A. (1986). Dropping out: How much do schools contribute to the problem? *Teachers College Record, 87,* 374–392.

Weinstein, C. S., & Mignano, A. (1993). *Elementary classroom management: Lessons from research and practice.* New York: McGraw-Hill.

Weinstien, R. S. (1989). Perception of classroom processes and student motivation: Children's views of self-fulfilling prophecies. In C. Ames & R. Ames (Eds.), *Research on motivation in education: Vol. 3. Goals and cognitions* (pp. 187–221). San Diego, CA: Academic Press.

Wlodkowski, R. J. (1991). *Motivation and teaching: A practical guide.* Washington, DC: National Education Association Press.

Woolfolk, A. E., & Hoy, W. K. (1990). Prospective teacher's sense of efficacy and beliefs about control. *Journal of Educational Psychology, 82,* 81–91.

Wubbels, T., & Levy, J. (1993). *Do you know what you look like? Interpersonal relationships in education.* Washington, DC: Falmer Press.

Zimmerman, B. J., & Martinez-Pons, M. (1988). Construct validation of a strategy model of student self-regulated learning. *Journal of Educational Psychology, 80*(3), 284–290.

ABOUT THE AUTHORS

Dale Scott Ridley is an assistant professor at the West Campus of Arizona State University in Phoenix, Arizona. He has a PhD in educational psychology from the University of Texas at Austin. He has 10 years of experience in teaching and research in the areas of teacher and student self-regulation and motivation. His particular area of expertise is strategies for reflective teaching and learning.

Bill Walther is a middle school teacher for Amphitheater Public School in Tucson, Arizona. He has a BA in education from the University of Arizona and is currently working on his master's degree in educational leadership. Bill has been teaching for 10 years and was recently named the Arizona Science Teacher of the Year for 1994 by the Arizona Science Teacher's Association. His particular area of expertise is using technology to enhance student learning and motivation.